A Psalm of Life

HENRY WADSWORTH LONGFELLOW

Tell me not, in mournful numbers,
Life is but an empty dream!
For the soul is dead that slumbers,
And things are not what they seem.

Life is real! Life is earnest!
And the grave is not its goal;
Dust thou art, to dust returnest,
Was not spoken of the soul.

Not enjoyment, and not sorrow,
Is our destined end or way;
But to act, that each to-morrow
Find us farther than to-day.

Art is long, and Time is fleeting,
And our hearts, though stout and brave,
Still, like muffled drums, are beating
Funeral marches to the grave.

In the world's broad field of battle,
In the bivouac of Life,
Be not like dumb, driven cattle!
Be a hero in the strife!

Trust no Future, howe'er pleasant!
Let the dead Past bury its dead!
Act,— act in the living Present!
Heart within, and God o'erhead!

Lives of great men all remind us
We can make our lives sublime,
And, departing, leave behind us
Footprints on the sands of time;

Footprints, that perhaps another,
Sailing o'er life's solemn main,
A forlorn and shipwrecked brother,
Seeing, shall take heart again.

Let us, then, be up and doing,
With a heart for any fate;
Still achieving, still pursuing,
Learn to labor and to wait.

Footprints
on the
Sands of Time:
Personal Reflections
on
Life and Death

By
Dr. Donald DeMarco

Footprints on the Sands of Time:
Personal Reflections on Life and Death

Design by James Kent Ridley

Published by Goodbooks Media

O Sapientia,
quae ex ore Altissimi prodidisti,
attingens a fine usque ad finem,
fortiter suaviter disponensque omnia:
veni ad docendum nos viam prudentiae.

ISBN-13: 978-1539570936

ISBN-10: 1539570932

3453 Aransas, Corpus Christi, Texas, 78411
www.goodbooksmedia.com

Dedication:

*This book is dedicated
to my parents, Marc and Rita,
in gratitude for the footprints they left behind.*

Acknowledgement:

Compiling a book is by no means a solitary enterprise. Therefore, I would like to express my sincere thanks to Peggy, Caitlin, Gretchen, Tom, and Roberta for their support and encouragement; Clare Adamo, librarian at Holy Apostles' College & Seminary, for her able assistance; my wife, Mary, who read each chapter with a critical eye; and James Ridley who continues to believe in the social significance of my writing.

TABLE OF CONTENTS

Part I: Reflections on Death

V The Death of Democracy

Part II: Reflections on Life

VI Living as a Person

VII Living a Life of Mercy

VIII Living a Life of Virtue

IX Living a Life of Freedom

X Living Life on the Horizon

INTRODUCTION

The expression, "Footprints on the Sands of Time," appears in Henry Wadsworth Longfellow's celebrated poem, *A Psalm of Life.* It represents an imaginative conjunction of life and death. Though we are mortal, we can leave footprints for succeeding generations. Thus, there is life in death. These footprints symbolize continuity and hope, as well as generosity and guidance. While we live, we know that we are running out of the grains of sand which have been allotted us. The realization that our time is limited should provide us with a strong incentive to do something to give our life meaning and to contribute to those who follow.

Novelist, musician, Anthony Burgess said it well, when he reminded us that "Wedged as we are between two eternities of idleness, there is no excuse to be idle now". Burgess, himself, was by no means idle. Before his sands ran out, he produced 33 novels, a staggering number of essays, poems, screenplays, children's books, biographies, and critical studies, as well as an impressive collection of songs and symphonies.

For St. Thomas Aquinas, man can find no rest in the lassitude of an idle life. A life of laziness is always a life of restlessness. It is only when a person gives himself to do God's work in life that he can enter into rest. We are given time to work, eternity to rest. The footprints that the Angelic Doctor has bequeathed to us are indeed deep and massive. They are both permanent and inspirational. We redeem our brief time on earth by transcending it through work.

Human existence is a mosaic of life and death. Without God and without hope, we enter death-in-life. With God and with hope, we find life-in-death. Our present epoch is marked, as Saint John Paul II has stated in his encyclical, *The Gospel of Life*, by a clash between a Culture of Life and a Culture of Death. The foregoing essays offer my personal reflections on how the surrounding gloom of a Culture of Death is discouraging many of us from living the kind of life that is not only our deepest source of meaning, but also our destiny and our beatitude. We should cherish life and discover ways, through knowledge and love, in which we can experience its rich rewards and to share them with others.

It is the author's hope that this work will deepen the reader's appreciation for life while better preparing him to avoid the seductions of death.

D. DeMarco
Kitchener, Ontario
June 8, 2016

PART ONE
REFLECTIONS ON DEATH

CHAPTER ONE
DEATH AND ITS VICTIMS

THE DEATH OF CELESTIAL BODIES

W e now know, thanks to the science of physics, that stars do perish. A star can exist in relative stability for billions of years, but eventually runs out of hydrogen. After that, when it exhausts its supply of the helium it has concocted through fusion, it runs out of fuel and "dies". One can hardly fault the ancients for believing that stars were imperishable. To the ancient Egyptians, the imperishable stars suggested a link between this world of mortality and a world of eternality. They seemingly offered evidence of life after death. Aristotle held that the stars were composed of a fifth element that was essentially different from air, earth, fire, and water. This fifth element, from which is derived the word "quintessence" (*quinta* + *essentia*), was, for the great philosopher, imperishable.

The ancients, however, were not entirely wrong. The human soul longs for eternity and has always been finding suggestions of it even in a world that is dying. Shakespeare referred to man as the "quintessence of dust". This raised the question of whether the soul of man, that which is "quintessential," is itself a sign of immortality. G. K. Chesterton used the image of the stars to suggest man's transcendent destiny: "If seeds in the black earth can turn into such beautiful roses, what might not the heart of man become in its long journey toward the stars?" Our world of shadows intimates a higher world of light. Are we human beings paradoxical creatures, composed of starlight and earth dust? We should never think, however, that the dust component is dominant. As Henry Wadsworth Longfellow has reminded us, "Dust thou art, to dust returnest, was not spoken of the soul" (*A Psalm of Life*).

We are mortal beings who have occasional glimpses into our immortality. For children, time moves so slowly that an entire summer can seem like an eternity. This is why Phyllis McGinley can interpret the bell of the Good Humor Man as heralding a life without end. It is a sound that makes the "promise plain to every comer: Unending sweets, imperishable summer." Yet summer passes, and each successive summer passes more swiftly than its predecessor, leaving older people to look elsewhere to find symbols of the imperishable. In his *Intimations of Immortality from Recollections of Early Childhood*, William Wordsworth laments the fact that "the radiance which was once so bright be now for ever taken from my sight" and seeks signs of meaning and immortality "In the faith that looks through death. In years that bring the philosophic mind."

We may no longer view stars, as did the ancients, as imperishable. But we do look at them as something on which we should hitch our wagons. Stars now symbolize success. When the great opera diva Geraldine Farrar once interrupted Arturo Toscanini during one of his famous outbursts, she insisted that he should not treat her so rudely since she is a star. The maestro's tart reply brought her back to earth, "Only the sky has stars". Toscanini was right, though we still cling to the notion that being a star grants us very special privileges. "Die? Asked the legendary movie star, John Barrymore. "I should say not, dear fellow. No Barrymore would allow such a conventional thing to happen to him." Barrymore passed away on May 29, 1942. His star status had not immunized him against that very conventional occurrence. Stars indeed perish, both the ones situated in the heavens as well as those crowned by Hollywood.

On the first day of creation, according to *Genesis*, God said, "Let there be light". And "God saw that the light was good, and he separated the light from the darkness." If stars appeared early in God's creation, perhaps it was to symbolize his own imperishability. But "light" was merely a stage. And what a stage it is! The sun, which is but a medium size star, comprises 99.9% of the solar system's mass. Nonetheless, it is man, not light, that is made in His image. We should not mistake the stage for the drama. Stars may remind us of our immortality, but it is what they awaken in us that is the source of everlasting life.

What man has in dignity far surpasses what stars have in magnitude. In the final analysis, it is quality, not quantity that counts. Stars cannot comprehend themselves. There is a second meaning to the word "light". It refers to that power of illumination that resides in the mind of man by which, as Aristotle says, he "can know all things". The universe would not be complete without a being, such as man, who could comprehend and enjoy the majesty and beauty of the cosmos. The stars are "light," but man is

16

"enlightened". Stars perish. Man prevails. This is the great cosmic paradox that puzzles physicists who see the universe as hastening, according to the Second Law of Thermodynamics, to eventual cosmic death. It is humble *Homo sapiens*, that outlasts the stars. The two exceedingly different factors that fascinated the philosopher Immanuel Kant were the "starry skies above" and "the moral law within". How could such disparate realities be in some way interconnected? Only the Creator could bring such seemingly antithetic factors into harmony with each other. Stars inspire us, and yet, in their own mysterious way, help us to understand that it is the Word of God and the soul of man that endure forever.

THE DEATH OF HOLLYWOOD CELEBRITIES

Death, we are told by a most reliable source, can come like a thief in the night. We are all mortal and even stars perish. The year dies at the close of December 31. We wonder how the New Year's child aged so much in just twelve months. As the year comes to an end, we think hopefully of the following year. Yet, we cannot forget the rapid passing of the current one. Death is all-embracing, even to those glamorous beings who are identified as "stars".

So many lives, vibrant on the screen, energetic on the playing field, refreshing as comedians, thriving as authors, and influential in the world of politics, have made their exits from the land of the living in the year of 2015. Even stars flicker, falter, and fall. Nonetheless, we always experience a certain shock, along with a respectful sadness when we learn of their demise. Did not Maureen O'Hara, Anita Ekberg, Leonard Nimoy, Omar Sharif, and Louis Jourdan appear to be immortal in celluloid? Yogi Berra, Ernie Banks, Frank Gifford, and Moses Malone, whose names were linked with "winning," are now numbered among the numberless who have lost their lives. Anne Meara and Judy Carne, who spread laughter, are now silent. Politics has said goodbye to Mario Cuomo, while Jackie Collins will never write another best-seller. We also said farewell to Rod Taylor, Dean Jones, and Dick Van Patten. We envied all those celebrities who seemed larger than life. And now we realize that they were as mortal as anyone else. Our envy has turned to sympathy, a more properly human emotion. In death we are united with them. We will miss their vitality. The strange and unexpected feeling comes over us that, at least for the present, we, the "non-celebrities," have outlived the "stars".

Death is the great leveler. Media immortality, if there can be such a thing, is not personal immortality. The various "stars" who performed so admirably on the world's stage, beguiled and entertained us. But they were not beings who belonged to the stratosphere. They were basically just like us, as it turns out – imperfect, fragile, and destined to pass from the earth.

Their deaths bring to mind two thoughts: that the distinction between celebrity and non-celebrity is trivial; that we must renew our commitment to finding meaning in our own lives and not in the accomplishments of others. We bid good-bye to Wes Craven, Lizabeth Scott, Darryl Dawkins, Ken Stabler, B. B. King, and that "beautiful mind," John Forbes Nash, Jr., and return to our own day-to-day obligations with stronger dedication. Life belongs to the living. There are no stars, only we earthlings. We would do well to heed the words of G. K. Chesterton: "If the seeds of the black earth can turn into such beautiful roses, what might not the heart of man become in its long journey toward the stars."

The existential philosopher, Nikolai Berdyaev has stated that "Death is the most profound and significant fact of life, raising the least of mortals above the mean commonplaces of life." If there were no death, he goes on to say, life would be meaningless and without hope. It is only through death that we can escape to a better world. "If life in our world continued forever, there would be no meaning in it." "The meaning of death", for Berdyaev, "is that there can be no eternity in time and that an endless temporal series would be meaningless." People who merely reach for the stars are not reaching high enough.

Celebrities are called "Stars" because they populate a haven of popularity. Because of the electronic Media they can be seen from anyplace and by anyone. Like stars, they appear to be constantly shining. They are both above and beyond us. They seem to be, as the Ancients believed stars to be, "imperishable". Their deaths prove this image to be an illusion. In the final analysis, what we all yearn for is not stardom, but God's Kingdom. Fame is a soap bubble. Christianity teaches us about the Resurrection, which is the victory of life over death. In addition, we are less likely to mistreat our neighbors when we see them as dying, even though that point of death belongs to an indeterminate moment in the future. Recognizing each person's mortality elicits in us a certain sympathy that casts aside any possible rancor or envy that we might harbor. When we visit a person who is bedridden in a hospital, our thoughts and actions are loving and supportive. We fight each other in moments when we fail to see each other as we really are, namely, mortal beings who are destined to die.

The "bell tolls for Thee," as John Donne has reminded us. We owe each other a profound sympathy inasmuch as we are all made of the same clay and are traveling toward that presently unknown moment when time and eternity intersect. Our attitude toward others would be more Christian if we saw them as dying, however slowly, and establish our relationship with them in accordance with both this fact and the reality of our own mortality.

We say adieu to our panoply of celebrities with the hope that their personal lives have earned them an eternity of everlasting joy with the God who is Life does not cease on the midnight hour. These former stars, like everyone else, are placed in the merciful hand of God.

THE DEATH OF THE SPOKEN WORD

A **person's last words**—his exit line—may or may not be his conscious good-bye to the world he is about to leave. They may or may not be characteristic of him, encapsulating his life in a few syllables. It is a romantic idea, however, to think that they are, like the dying words of an actor. Hamlet's last words were, "the rest is silence". Julius Caesar's last words were, Et tu, Brute? Then fall Caesar." What could be more theatrical? On the other hand, Scarlett O'Hara's last words in *Gone With the Wind*—"Tomorrow is another day"—are bright with hope and determination. Her words parallel in optimism the final words of Sidney Carton as he faced execution in Charles Dickens' *A Tale of Two Cities*: "It is a far, far better thing I do, than I have ever done; it is a far, far better rest that I go to than I have ever known."

We cherish the notion of saving the best for the last: the walk-off homerun, the winning basket at the buzzer, the game-winning touchdown in the dying seconds of the game. We like fireworks at the end of a public event. We enjoy the dazzling finale of a great symphony. We bid a warm goodbye to friends as an appropriate closure to our time spent together. The day ends in darkness; life ends with either hope or despair. Christ's Last Words, "Father, into your hands I commend my spirit" (Luke 23:46) give us pause. They were fitting and indicated that death is not final. They imply an end that is more truly a beginning. So, too, the last words of the dying year welcome the New Year.

What is last is by no means least. If we do not utter appropriate words at the close of our life, we should have appropriate thoughts. But life can be ambiguous to some people. Marlon Brando once stated that when it came time for him to take his last breath he would say to himself, "What was that all about?" In the style of his profession, Alfred Hitchcock's dying words were: "One never knows the ending. One has to die to know exactly what happens after death, although Catholics have their hopes." Archbishop of

Canterbury, Thomas à Becket's final words expressed less ambiguity: "I am ready to die for my Lord, that in my blood the Church may obtain liberty and peace."

While a priest was reading Charlie Chaplin his last rites, he recited the words, "May the Lord have mercy on your soul." "Why not?", was the legendary actor's reply, "After all, it belongs to him." When I relayed this anecdote to a priest friend of mine, he responded with an immediate burst of enthusiasm: "How wonderful!" he exclaimed. There must be some theological depth to Chaplin's reply, I thought, since it prompted such a strong and spontaneous affirmation.

It does not matter that the exchange between the priest and the revered actor might not have really taken place since the same exchange occurs in the 1947 movie, *Monsieur Verdoux*. Be that as it may, it was the rich theological implications that interested me.

Our soul does, indeed, belong to the God who created it. Thus, God is most inclined to have mercy on something of his own making. We can, therefore, expect mercy from Him. And yet, we are in charge of our soul. It is "ours" in the sense that it is entrusted to us. We are the stewards of our soul. And when we meet our Maker, He will review what we have done with it.

Joan Crawford, who specialized in portraying characters that were often self-centered and cold blooded, had a different exit line. When, on her death bed, she overheard her housekeeper praying aloud for her, she said, rather forcefully, "Don't you dare ask God to help me." Ms. Crawford may have felt that her soul belonged exclusively to herself.

What we have done with the soul that God has entrusted to us is the subject of our final examination. We can expect mercy, but we must show God how much we appreciated his gift to us. When we return the rental to the car dealer, we may have to pay for whatever damages it sustained while we were using it.

"May the Lord have mercy on your soul" is spoken, and properly so, in the subjunctive mood. God will have mercy on our souls only if we are willing to accept it, and perhaps more importantly, if we have shown mercy to others.

Yet there is another factor. We are terribly fallible creatures, prone to an endless series of crimes and follies. God is merciful to us because of His loving generosity; but He is also merciful to us because He is sympathetic to our wounded condition. "Heaven have mercy on us all," wrote the great American novelist, Herman Melville, "for we are all somehow dreadfully cracked about the head and sadly need mending."

God's mercy is available, but it is not administered unless a person wills to receive it. Water is abundantly available. But a person may choose not to utilize it to wash his face. The moment of death is one of intense realism. "So then, you will know them by their fruits. Not everyone who says to Me, 'Lord, Lord,' will enter the kingdom of heaven, but he who does the will of my Father who is in heaven will enter" (Matthew 7:21).

One prays that God's bounteous mercy will shine on the good fruits of a person's life and that the combination of mercy and goodness will illuminate the pathway to a better world.

THE DEATH OF A PERSON

Aristotle, as a good philosopher, understood the importance of thinking. In fact, he valued it so highly that he accorded it a divine status. His God was primarily a thinker. But he was a God whose object of thought was nothing other than Himself. He did not, owing to His grandeur, think of anyone else.

Rene Descartes, the father of Modern Philosophy, also thought very highly of thinking. He enshrined it at the very beginning of philosophy. But somewhat like his Greek predecessor, his act of thinking did nothing other than affirm his existence. His thinking was self-contained.

For most people, being the object of the thoughts of others is very important. People do not want to be forgotten. They want to be remembered, even after death. In Andrew Lloyd Webber's popular musical *The Phantom of the Opera*, he has Christine say to Raoul, "Think of me, think of me fondly when we've said goodbye. Remember me, once in a while. Please, promise me once in a while. Please, promise me you'll try." Being thoughtful of others is considered a great virtue. By contrast, thoughtlessness is universally disparaged.

Why is it so important for people to be thought about and remembered? Why is it so important to be kept alive in the mind of others? It may seem like an unwarranted leap of the imagination, but it may be that we owe our very being to someone who thought kindly enough about us to bring us into existence. The desire to be thought of may be a reminiscence that goes back to our first experience as a creature. Being thought of is an even earlier experience than being warmed by our mother's love. We come "from afar, not in entire forgetfulness," as the poet states. There is an imprint on our soul, like our need to love, that cannot be completely effaced.

Pope Benedict XVI, as Cardinal Ratzinger, has written about *anamnesis* (using Plato's term) which is something like an original memory that is implanted in "the ground of our existence". "This *anamnesis* of the origin," he writes, "results from the god-like constitution of our being," representing "a store of retrievable contents." In other words, we remain in touch, however dimly, with certain aspects of our being that God impressed in us at the moment of our creation. God thought of us when He made us. *Anamnesis* may retrieve the memory of that thought-to-being moment. Hence, we love to be thought of in a positive way, the original experience being the prototype of all our similar and subsequent experiences. For Joseph Ratzinger, the Gospel "must be proclaimed to the pagans, because they themselves are yearning for it in the inner recesses of their souls." The Gospel, therefore, does not impose, it awakens us to who we are in a most profound way.

The Judaeo-Christian God is also a thinker. But his thinking is anything but self-contained. He thinks of others. The object of his thinking is someone other than Himself. He is a generous thinker. In fact, He is so generous a thinker that He thinks of people even before they exist. In fact, His thinking brings them into existence. If God stopped thinking of us, we would cease to exist.

In his first homily as pope, Benedict XVI stated that "We are not some casual and meaningless product of evolution. Each of us is the result of a thought of God. Each of us is willed, each of us is loved, each of us is necessary." We think of God as a Creator. But there are some important adjectives that attach to His creative act. First of all, He is a thoughtful Creator. We do not come about by chance. Our existence was preceded by God's thoughtfulness. There is a purpose to our existence. Secondly, His thoughtfulness is characterized by love. And if God wills our existence out of His loving thoughtfulness, who is going to stop Him? Therefore, His creation of each one of us individual human beings is necessary.

There is much talk these days about "reproductive freedom". No human being, however, has the capability of determining that this particular child and not that particular child be conceived. A woman carries hundreds of thousands of ova, while a man carries millions of spermatozoa. Which spermatozoon fertilizes which egg is not an event over which any human being has determinative power. "Before I formed you in the womb I knew you," we read in Jeremiah 1:5. In her Diary, St. Faustina records the words that Jesus spoke to her: "I thought of you before I called you into being . . . before I made the world, I loved you with the love your heart is experiencing today, and, throughout the centuries, My love will never change."

I came across an advertisement recently for a collection of Canadian postage stamps. The seller fixed his price at $38,000. He agreed to provide pictures of the stamps on request. The pictures, of course, would be worth nothing. The actual stamps command a lofty prices because there are the originals; the pictures are merely copies. We human beings have high value (ontological value not market value) because of our origin with God. We are not copies of copies of copies, etc., which is the position that the atheistic evolutionist must hold. God is intimately involved in our creation at its origin. We are originals!

God created us thoughtfully and lovingly. We sense this whenever we are touched by the loving thoughtfulness of others. At such moments we remember, however vaguely, the truth and goodness of this experience that goes back to our origin. We say, "Thank you," an expression that is derived from "thinking". Old English word *thanc* means "kindly thought. The words for "thank" in German and Dutch, *Dank* and *dank*, respectively, also mean "to think".

God is a thoughtful Creator. When we thank another for his thoughtfulness, we are behaving in a God-like fashion.

THE DEATH OF A LOVED ONE

Should Old Aquinas be forgot and never brought to mind? Rather, he should be well remembered because he helps to form the mind. This is sufficient reason to remember and honor him on his January 28th Feast Day. Apart from being a philosopher and theologian of unparalleled excellence, he, along with William Shakespeare, stands among the greatest psychologists of Western history. A good example of the Angelic Doctor's psychological acumen can be found in his *Summa Theologica* (I-II, Q. 38, a.3) where he presents five remedies for pain and sorrow. Since pain and sorrow enter the lives of everyone born into this valley of tears, these remedies have great practical significance and should be of widespread interest. What is more is that they all have the virtues of being natural, readily available, cost-free, and devoid of side effects.

The first of his quintet of remedies is delectation (or pleasure). Aquinas reasons that pain or sorrow result from causes that are not natural to the human appetites which, of themselves, are ordered to something good. Pleasure, on the other hand, "is a kind of repose of the appetite in a suitable good." Therefore, because pleasure is, in this way, the opposite of pain and sorrow, which is a kind of "weariness," it can assuage them. Food at a funeral, for example, can assist in relieving the sorrow caused by the loss of a loved one.

The second remedy Aquinas lists is tears (and also other outward expressions such as groans and spoken words). He offers two reasons that explain why tears can assuage pain or sorrow. The first is based on the notion that something hurtful hurts all the more "if we keep it shut up". Weeping is an escape route for pain and sorrow in a way that lessens their torment. "Tears and groans," he writes, "naturally assuage sorrow". The second reason is that any good action is a source of pleasure since it demonstrates that the sufferer is at least doing something to alleviate his condition.

Remedy number three is the compassion of friends. Sorrow has a depressing effect and tends to weigh a person down. The compassion of friends tends to pick a person up, lighten his burden as if these friends "were bearing the burden with him, striving, as it were, to lessen its weight". Yet, for Aquinas, a more important reason has to do with the love his friends manifest. The recognition of this love offers a kind of blessing that mitigates the sufferer's burden. He takes heart, so to speak, when he witnesses the love that others have for him. As Shakespeare writes in *Timon of Athens*, "A friend should bear his friend's infirmities."

The fourth remedy is the least corporeal and most spiritual. It is the contemplation of truth. This remedy works "the more perfectly," as St. Thomas notes, the more "one is a lover of wisdom". In the contemplation of Divine things," we are drawn to a higher region where God alone knows why certain difficulties and afflictions have arisen. We may not know exactly why certain torments occur, but the thought that God has His reasons is a source of consolation and comfort. The contemplation of truth can also be a source of pleasure, just as knowledge is a source of pleasure.

Aquinas' final remedies are sleep and baths. He reasons that remedies that are good and natural for the body tend "to bring nature back to its normal state." Sleep and bathing help to restore nature's equilibrium. Pain and sorrow are naturally "repugnant to the vital movement of the body." Therefore, the natural pleasures associated with sleep and baths offer a certain recovering pleasure. In *Macbeth*, Shakespeare offers a virtual hymn to sleep's natural benefits: "Sleep that knits up the raveled sleeve of care," that is "sore labor's bath, balm for hurt minds, great nature's second course," and "the chief nourisher in life's feast." In the words of St. Ambrose, "Sleep restores the tired limbs to labor, refreshes the weary mind, and banishes sorrow."

Aquinas, Doctor of the Church, is also a Doctor of Common Sense. He understands the nature of the body as well as the nature of the human being. He is more practical than theoretical, more clear and direct, than abstruse and academic. His thought, though he lived and wrote in the 13th century, is permanent. He is to philosophy and theology what Michelangelo is to sculpture, what Beethoven is to music, what Leonardo is to painting, and what Sir Isaac Newton is to physics.

In our present technological society, our first thoughts concerning the alleviation of pain and sorrow are often products that are not natural but commercial. We reach for Aleve, Advil, Tylenol, and other pain killers, sometimes ignoring natural remedies that can be quite effective. It is well documented that tranquilizers and the like are highly over-prescribed. Aquinas would not oppose the use of synthetic drugs, but he would not want us to ignore natural remedies.

The Catholic Church has not forgotten St. Thomas. A more recent saint, Saint John Paul II, has reminded us that "the Church has been justified in consistently proposing St. Thomas as master of thought and a model of the right way to do theology." We are on firm ground when we listen to what one saint has to say about another saint.

CHAPTER TWO
THE DEATH OF THINKING

FEAR OF PRECISION

My biology teacher of many moons ago took perverse delight in terrorizing his students while they were taking an exam. "Plagiarism," he would bellow, "is arousing the suspicion of the proctor." He enjoyed the sound of his own voice and repeated this warning many times. He intended it to be more intimidating than cautionary. I found it to be as amusing, however, and remained confident that a mere flicker of suspicion was never going to convict anyone of the heinous crime of plagiarism. At the same time, I realized that our watchful supervisor was giving unaccustomed breadth to the word "plagiarism," imbuing it with a far-reaching application so that it could indict both the guilty and the innocent in the same breath.

Words are defined. This is the essential purpose of the dictionary. This means that they have boundaries. Their boundaries set apart from each other what the word means and what is does not mean, just as my fence delineates where my backyard ends and where that of my neighbor's begins. "Left" does not mean "right"; nor does "right" mean "left". Every word is, at the same time, exclusive as well as inclusive. In thinking back on my old biology professor, I now see that he was ahead of his time, allowing a word to break out of its dictionary definition and extend to what the word was never supposed to reach. His over-extended use of the word "plagiarism" did not worry me. What worries me in the contemporary world is how this same disregard for the integrity of the word is being practiced by government leaders and members of the Supreme Court.

Paul Martin, former Prime Minister of Canada told the press that he legalized same-sex marriage because, as a lawyer, he was obliged to interpret the law as broadly as possible. Edmund Burke, on the other hand, established a more sensible shibboleth for lawyers to follow when he stated that "Law sharpens the mind by narrowing it." In jurisprudence, one does not convict, out of zeal for being broad, all the suspects, but narrows the list until he finds the one who is guilty. Thinking is a narrowing activity. It separates what is true from what is false, the evidence from the hearsay, what is relevant from what is irrelevant. When we over-extend the meaning of marriage we begin to apply it to something that is not marriage.

President Obama enthusiastically supports marriage of the same-sex variety because, as he puts it, it allows you to be "free to marry who [sic] you love." No doubt this is a broader use of the word marriage than the President intended since it would include parents marrying their children and siblings marrying each other. But when we stretch the meaning of word beyond its limits, how do we know when to stop? The press has reported about a lonely cowboy who wants to marry his horse.

John McKellar, a self-identified "openly gay male," founded an organization in 1997 called HOPE (Homosexuals Opposed to Pride Extremism). He is fully respectful of the meaning of marriage that includes the four prohibitions that distinguish what marriage is from what marriage is not: "you can only marry one person at a time, only someone of the opposite sex, never someone beneath a certain age, and not a close blood relative." Homosexuals have the same right to marriage as heterosexuals, but each must abide by the four prohibitions.

Closely allied with the hyperinflation of the word "marriage" is a similar expansion of the words "bigot" and "discrimination". The former word, freed from its reference to a stubbornly intolerant or prejudiced person, now extends to anyone who defends traditional marriage. Presumably, anyone from Moses to John McKellar is a bigot. "Discrimination" is no longer restricted to unjust discrimination but now includes making virtually any distinction whatsoever. Hence, it is alleged to be discriminatory against women to ban them from a barbershop quartet, or discriminatory against atheists to schedule a formal prayer at a Catholic University. By logical extension, everyone becomes a bigot and any distinction whatsoever constitutes discrimination. The balloon expands when inflated until it bursts. The rubber band stretches when pulled until it snaps. Words, too, have their limitations. They cease to be true to their meaning when their limitations are not respected.

Words should remain connected with thought in order to stimulate thinking. To isolate the word from thought is to deprive it of its purpose. Samuel Johnson once remarked that "One of the disadvantages of wine is to make a man mistake words for thought." Political correctness can function as a verbal intoxicant. Disconnected from thought, words becomes "weasel words," "buzz words," "spin words," or simply "gobbledygook". This makes dialogue and discussion impossible. Dr. Johnson preferred sober personal exchanges: "That is the happiest conversation where there is no competition, no vanity, but a calm quiet interchange of sentiments."

Words are conveyors of thought. They should sharpen the mind, not dull it. Most unfortunately, the modern world is turning them into the equivalent of traffic signs that prompt automatic responses. Marriage, bigotry, and discrimination are words that are too important to be deprived of their avenues to thought. How serious is the matter? We are advised in Matthew 12:36 that "Every idle word that men shall speak, they shall give account thereof in the day of judgment."

FEAR OF ALIENATION

There are two popular maxims to live by that, taken together, provide not clarity but confusion. The first advises us to "think outside the box". This bromide appeals to our sense of independence. We are flattered into believing that we are bold and adventurous and will not be confined to a way of life that is prescribed by others. This has proven to be a most effective maxim, but only in achieving widespread acceptance. The second one is "get with the program". In this case, the appeal is to our sense of community. We think it is arrogant to believe that we can invent our own program, while rejecting what has already been established with our good in mind. We are reluctant to abandon the time-tested for the unproven. Like the first maxim, it, too, has achieved popularity, but without success.

The first maxim strokes our ego; the second touches out humility. Although each is trendy and popular, they both dispense with thinking while perfectly contradicting each other. They hoodwink us into believing that a mere slogan is more illuminating than thinking. They promise to make life easier for us, but their passport to simplicity is counterfeit.

The thinking person would want to know what is in the box as well as being aware of what makes up the program. Not wanting to know what is in the box or anything about the program is to avoid thinking. As a teacher, I always want my students to know that if they are catching opinions, they may be catching them the way that one catches a cold: they are thrust upon them.

Thinking does not permit excessive short cuts. It abhors the one-dimensional command. Haste may make waste, but a stitch in time still saves nine. Slogans are handy, but they lack breadth. They are attractive to the mentally indolent. Thinking takes time, something that many people seem to have in scarce supply.

I recall asking a class of fifty students for a description of "peace" that is more positive than "the absence of war". No one could provide me with anything that went beyond the usual negativity: "the avoidance of hostility," "the removal of stress," "the freedom from worry," etc. Their peace offerings failed to inform me of what peace is. I suggested that negative definitions are not illuminating. We would not say that a "man" is simply "not a woman" or that "life" is merely "not being dead". Mother Teresa was once asked why she did not participate in anti-war demonstrations. She said that "I will never do that, but as soon as you have a pro-peace rally, I'll be there."

Finally, in order to make my question more down to earth and less abstract, I asked them what they might do if they wanted to find, sometime within the next week, ten minutes of peace. Philosophy does have a practical side to it. Silence prevailed for some time, until one student explained, disconsolately, that given her busy schedule, finding ten minutes to experience peace was, at least for several weeks, completely out of the question.

Poet and essayist Don Marquis, has made the remark that "If you make people think that they're thinking, they'll love you; but if you really make them think, they'll hate you." Of course, being a teacher is not the same thing as being a demagogue. On the other hand, "really making students think" could adversely affect my student-teacher evaluations. Nonetheless, Marquis has a point. According to Rev. Martin Luther King, Jr., "Rarely do we find men who willingly engage in hard, solid thinking. There is an almost universal quest for easy answers and half-baked solutions. Nothing pains some people more than having to think." The reverend King is wisely distinguishing "solid thinking" from "wishful thinking". We all wish things were better. But nothing improves when wishes supplant thinking.

A good philosopher is a good example of a good thinker. According to St. Augustine, "Peace is the tranquility of order". For Benedict Spinoza, "Peace is not the absence of war: it is a virtue born of the strength of the heart". Alfred North Whitehead referred to peace as "A trust in the efficacy of beauty." In these positive explanations of peace we find food for thought: Peace requires an inner disposition that is in harmony with the outer world. It is founded on a "strength of the heart" that trusts the order and beauty of things. Peace is experienced when the virtuous person comes to terms with his life and his surroundings in a mood of tranquility. Thinking about peace is an important step toward experiencing it.

Examples of non-thinking in our present culture abound: Contraception is simply responsible sex, abortion is merely a choice, euthanasia is just death with dignity, same-sex marriage is nothing more than a civil right, while traditional marriage is legalized slavery. In these examples, thinking is truncated so that automatic responses can prevail. It is precisely because man is a rational animal, however, that he cannot be free unless he is willing to think.

St. Paul is a model for the thinking person. In *Philippians* 4:8, he makes the following entreaty: "Finally, brothers and sisters, whatever is true, whatever is noble, whatever is right, whatever is pure, whatever is lovely, whatever is admirable—if anything is excellent or praiseworthy—think about such things."

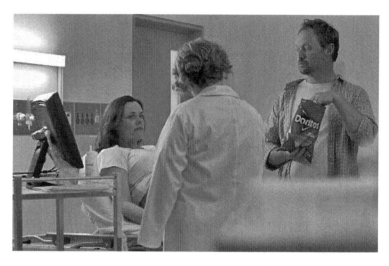

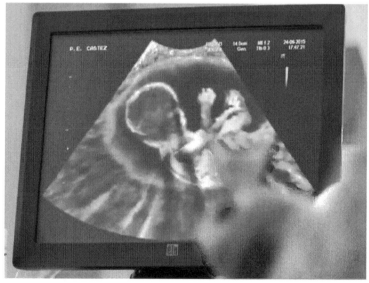

FEAR OF SCIENCE

Science can be inconvenient, even troubling, to those who prefer living by mythology. We find an example of this in the reaction of the National Abortion Rights Action League (NARAL) over a thirty second commercial that showed a mother getting an ultrasound at nine months. In the commercial, the OB/GYN tells the mother that the baby is due any day. Meanwhile, the expectant father is waving a single nacho cheese Dorito over the child's belly. The monitor shows that the baby is moving with the motion of the chip. This was enough to outrage the so-called "pro-choice" group that perceived the advertisement to exemplify "anti-choice tactics of humanizing fetuses".

NARAL would prefer to live in a world of its own creation. The commercial does not humanize the fetus; it acknowledge what science reports, namely that the unborn child is already part of the human family. Through ultrasound, science has opened a window into the life of the unborn and has some extraordinary things to report. If there is one area in which we can say that there is progress, it is the area of our vastly improved knowledge of the unborn child.

Boris Brott is one of the most internationally recognized Canadian symphony conductors. He holds major positions as music director in both Canada and the United States. Presently, he enjoys an international career as guest conductor, educator, motivational speaker, and cultural ambassador. He has something quite fascinating to tell us about life in the womb.

In a radio interview, he was once asked how he became interested in music. It seemed to be a typical question and the interviewer probably expected a typical answer. Brott's response, however, was both unexpected and illuminating. "You know, this may sound strange," he said, "but music has been a part of me since before birth." He went on to explain. Somehow, I knew the cello line of scores I was conducting before I had ever seen them. He mentioned this to his mother who was a professional cellist and

enumerated all the pieces he seemed to know before he had ever seen them. His mother had an answer for this apparent mystery. She had played all these pieces while she was pregnant with him. Brott had a head start as a musician even before he was born.

Examples of pre-natal learning are numerous. An American mother who had lived in Toronto during her pregnancy overheard her two-year-old daughter chanting, "Breathe in, breathe out, breathe in, breathe out." The mother recognized the words as part of her Lamaze exercise. But the child could not have picked them up from watching television since she was now living in Oklahoma City, and the words she was uttering were unique to the Canadian version of the Lamaze exercise.

Tom Verny, is a distinguished psychiatrist who has taught at several universities including Harvard, and the University of Toronto. His book, *The Secret Life of the Unborn Child*, has become a bestseller, and is published in 27 countries. His contribution to scientific literature is most impressive. As a result of several years of research, Verny concludes that "The fetus can see, hear, experience, taste and, on a primitive level, even learn in utero (that is, in the uterus—before birth). Most importantly, he can feel—not with an adult's sophistication, but feel nonetheless." Therefore, as a corollary, Verny maintains, while a mother is carrying her child, life-enhancing emotions, such as joy, elation and the anticipation of delivering her child, can contribute significantly to the emotional development of the child.

NARAL, by allowing itself to be "outraged" by the ultrasound image of an unborn child as depicted in a television commercial, is showing itself to be more anti-science than pro-choice. Surely a scientist should be pro-science without having to make apologies to anyone. Such outrage, of course, is used to protect a rather feeble ideology, one that begins with the indefensible assumption that the unborn child is not an unborn child. The scientific evidence for the humanity of the unborn child, however, is conclusive. If we want to live in reality, we cannot ignore hard facts and continue to hide in a mythological world of our own invention.

FEAR OF LOSS

Maggie Gallagher, in her 1995 book, *The Abolition of Marriage: How We Lost the Right to a Lasting Love*, made the following ominous statement: "The evidence is now overwhelming that the collapse of marriage is creating a whole generation of children less happy, less physically and mentally healthy, less equipped to deal with life or produce at work, and more dangerous to themselves and others." Divorce, out-of-wedlock pregnancies, single-parent families, and broken homes are not in the best interest of children.

Twenty years later, as if to design a plan to make things even worse, *Obergefell v. Hodges* denied the importance to a child of having a mother and a father. In retrospect, it should not be surprising that the United States Supreme Court that could, as a consequence of *Roe v. Wade*, consign tens of millions of unborn children to premature death, would have any regard for future children who would not be aborted. The 1973 and 2015 Courts were in love with liberty, but not, as they should have been, with justice.

Our first obligation in justice to anything is to honor what it is. Now, any particular thing has a nature which defines what it is. Its nature also defines what it is not. G. K. Chesterton comments in his *Orthodoxy* that "the essence of every picture is the frame". By that he means that a thing's limitations are not handicaps, but are inseparable from its essence or nature. He advises us "not to go about as a demagogue, encouraging triangles to break out of the prison of their three sides. If a triangle breaks out of its three sides, its life comes to a lamentable end." The rubber band breaks when it is stretched too far; the balloon bursts when it is over-inflated. Man cannot be God; a horse cannot sing like a nightingale. We cannot pull ourselves up by our bootstraps. The limitations in every thing should not be seen as restrictions, but as defining properties. Chesterton cites a book entitled *The Loves of the Triangles*, which he confesses never to have read. But, as he remarks, "if triangles were ever loved, they were loved for being triangular."

The fatal flaw in the recent Supreme Court decision lies in its failure to recognize the nature of marriage, and its consequent identification of the very limits that give marriage its meaning as restrictions that should be withdrawn. Thus, five justices believed that by removing one of the essential factors of marriage to accommodate the wishes of same-sex couples, they would enlarge it. The truth is, that by flagrantly disregarding the nature of marriage, particularly the male/female requirement, they embarked on a course of action to disparage, if not to destroy it.

Marriage is defined in terms of several factors that distinguish it from any other forms of human alliance. It requires the mutual consent between two people who are unmarried, have no blood ties to each other, are of appropriate ages, and are members of the opposite sex. Consider the American "National Gay Rights Platform" put forward in 1972 (endorsed by Canadian homosexuals) that called for: a) the abolition of all laws governing 'age of sexual consent,' thus enabling adults to have sex with consenting children of any age or either sex; 2) the repeal of all laws against sodomy and adult or child prostitution; 3) the repeal of all laws that restrict the sex or number of persons entering into a marriage unit. Traditional marriage is not marriage in its abbreviated or abridged form. It is real marriage. The same cannot be said for same-sex unions.

William D. Gardner sees fit to include these points in his book, *The War Against the Family*, because he wants to tell the world of "The terribly destructive effect of the homosexual lobby on our most treasured moral and social institutions." What the *Platform* proposes as "marriage" is decidedly not marriage. What it proposes does not expand marriage, but seeks to replace it.

According to Justice Anthony Kennedy, "the right to marry is a fundamental right inherent in the liberty of the person . . . couples of the same-sex may not be deprived of this right and that liberty". What Kennedy ignores in the majority decision of *Obergefell v. Hodges* is the very nature of marriage which is a social institution and not something that arises within an individual person. In other words, a person's right to marry is conditioned by all the factors that constitute marriage. It is not a private option. Nor is it absolute. There are many heterosexual individuals in the world who would dearly love to marry, but they have no right to get married solely on their own merits. In some cases, it is impossible for them to marry. A right must, at the very least, be related to a possibility. Marriage is a conditional right, not a sovereign right. We do a grave injustice to marriage by denying what it is, then creating a fraudulent image of it, and finally presenting it to the world as an improvement. Liberty is not liberty when it negates both reason and reality. It is a mere velleity that has neither substance nor life.

FEAR OF TRUTH

If Mortimer Adler, after writing his classic, *How to Read a Book,* authored *How to Read the Newspaper,* he probably would have warned his readers that newspapers convey something other than news. They convey, he would advise, propaganda carefully concealed within what the inattentive reader might assume to be mere news. Consider the following three newspaper items culled recently from the same newspaper.

Gretta Vosper, an ordained minister of the United Church of Canada, has declared that she believes neither in God nor in the Bible. When she decided to abandon the Lord's Prayer, 100 of the 150 members of her congregation left in protest. She claims that belief in God can motivate bad things. Rev. Vosper has expressed "shock" that her position is now under review since, as she states, her congregants support her view that how you live is more important than what you believe. The board chairman who hired her says that he has had no complaints from congregants and avers that people enjoy engaging in critical thinking as they explore new ways of expressing their faith and values. The 57-year-old Rev. Vosper is depicted in the newspaper as flashing an engaging smile, an image that will win her support against the an alleged conservative elite that opposes "rich and alive" discussions. Her being "victimized" is sure to win her national sympathy.

The notion that how you live is more important than what you believe is deceptive since how one lives is based on what one believes. A person acts in accordance with his beliefs. Take away those beliefs and a person will not know how to act. In one sense, the fruit is more important than the seed. Yet, if there is no seed, there is not fruit. Moreover, Vosper was given the responsibility of preaching Gospel values. The fact that she has rejected them has not, at this point, led to her dismissal, but to her status as a national celebrity who has shown the gumption to stand for her own values. The message of liberal autonomy over-rides ministerial integrity.

An Ontario Court has upheld a lower court ruling not to accredit an evangelical Christian law school. The reason for denying accreditation is the school's policy that forbids students from having sex outside of marriage. The Court ruled that Trinity Western University failed "to balance the applicants' rights to freedom of religion with the equality rights of its future members from two historically disadvantaged minorities (LGBTQ persons and women)." According to the Court, the law school's policy discriminated against these minority groups: "in order to attend TWU (LGBTQ persons) must sign a document in which they agree to essentially bury a crucial component of their very identity, by forsaking any form of intimacy with those persons with whom they wish to form a relationship."

Neither gender nor sexual inclination disqualifies a person from being a Christian. Trinity Western's Christian mandate does not discriminate against anyone. Nor does it violate anyone's freedom. Any person has the freedom to enrol or not enrol in the law school. Furthermore, people are equally free to attend a school that, consistent with its Christian values, prohibits sexual intimacy apart from marriage. What appears to be discriminatory is not allowing a Christian school to operate according to its own Christian mandate. The issue of minorities is a red herring.

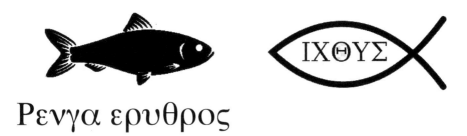

Ρεγγα ερυθρος

Certainly women do not constitute a "minority". No doubt there are other minorities for whom the school's policy is not an issue. In addition, can it be said that sexual intimacy is any more crucial to the identities of LGBTQ persons than it is for heterosexual people? Here, the Court is, in the interest of equality, ruling in favor of inequality. Once again, the veiled message is that certain people, because they are allegedly victims, should enjoy preferential treatment.

The Canadian Centre for Bio-ethical Reform has been mailing out flyers to residents of Saskatoon, Saskatchewan that include a picture of an aborted fetus and one of Prime Minister hopeful Justin Trudeau. The flyers, packaged within a white envelope that reads, "Important Election Information Enclosed," state that the candidate for the country's highest office supports abortion until birth and that "a vote for Justin Trudeau is a vote for this (referring to the aborted fetus)." Postal workers have complained about the "violent, graphic material" that they are delivering which, they believe, is contrary to "family values". Some of the postal workers have balked at delivering the flyers.

The real violence is the abortion of unborn children, not its depiction. The message contained in the flyers is truthful and even educational. If there is any threat to family values it is the deliberate destruction of one of its members, not that a young person (who may be witnessing violent images courtesy of the media on a daily basis) might see a picture of an aborted fetus. The Centre is presented as "anti-abortion" rather than "pro-life". It is painted as dangerous, as opposed to the complaining postal workers who are honorifically portrayed as being opposed to disseminating images of graphic violence and in favor of protecting family values. Once again, we find an inversion of values wherein the responsible people are presented as being irresponsible while the dubious complainers are vested with praise.

The distinguished American novelist James Fenimore Cooper was not only being unusually insightful but uncommonly prophetic when he penned these words in the *American Democrat*: "As the press of this country now exists, it would seem to be expressly devised by the great agent of mischief, to depress and destroy all that is good, and to elevate and advance all that is evil in the nation. The little truth that is urged, is usually urged coarsely, weakened and rendered vicious by personalities; while those who live by falsehoods, fallacies, enmities, partialities and the schemes of the designing, find in the press the very instrument that the devils would invent to effect their designs." What more can be added to that perspicacious remark than "amen"?

CHAPTER THREE
THE DEATH OF LANGUAGE

GIBBERISH

Gibberish is not restricted to merely speaking unintelligibly. It can be fine-honed into the art of saying something that seems to make sense, but makes no sense whatsoever. The success of gibberish depends on how the mere sound of words can have a mesmerizing effect on the listener even though they do not pass from the ear to the brain. It is the hypnotic sound of the words, not their meaning, which is the final test of artful gibberish.

Gertrude Stein was a pioneer in the art of gibberish. In her book, *Tender Buttons*, a work that is more discussed than read, she offers innumerable examples of her curious craft. One citation is sufficient to make the point: "The care with which the rain is wrong and the green is wrong and the white is wrong, the care with which there is a chair and plenty of breathing. The care with which there is incredible justice and likeness, all this makes a magnificent asparagus, and also a fountain." As the Bard might say, "Full of sound and fury, signifying nothing."

Marshall McLuhan, the eminent student of how the Media affects people without informing them, found a parallel between Stein's gibberish and Madison Avenue's commercials. Old cigarette ads provide ample illustrations of how statements can persuade consumers without informing them. An L & M cigarette commercial was able to convince many smokers that if they chose this brand, they would "Live Modern". At the same time, another brand claimed that "Only Chesterfield is made the modern way—with Accu-Ray". Not only that, a Chesterfield cigarette "packs more pleasure because it's more perfectly packed." Lucky Strike did not mean what the phrase denoted, but meant "fine tobacco". Moreover, they were "so round, so firm, so fully packed - so free and easy on the draw." Nonetheless, all these claims were summarily dismissed by another popular brand: "Have real cigarette – have a Camel."

Lewis Carroll wrote gibberish, not so much for monetary gain, but for the pleasure that meaningless words provided. In *Through the Looking Glass* he offers a delectable example of gibberish in the opening stanza of "Jabberwocky": "'Twas brilling, and the slithy toves/ Did gyre and gimble in the wabe:/ All mimsy were the borogoves,/ And the mome raths outgabe." Carroll's intention, however, was not to deceive, but to delight. It is an entirely different matter, however, when politicians utilize jibberish in order to mesmerize their audience.

Jennifer Rubin, in a *Washington Post* article entitled, "Hillary Clinton Spews Gibberish, Again", (October, 9, 2014), finds that the Democratic candidate for president "once more is saying nothing and using many words to say it, as if she is pulling buzz words and talking points from the recesses of her memory." To illustrate her point, she offers Clinton's comment on the Obama medical device tax: "On the tax itself, again I think we have to look to see what are the pluses and the minuses, that are embodied in a decision about either to remove or alter or continue this particular piece of the Affordable Care Act and I've [sic] in preparation for coming here, I've obviously looked at the arguments on both sides for more information and I think we'll gather more information and that will perhaps give us a better path forward."

According to journalist Michael Kelly, many of Hillary's speeches "share the same traits: vaulting ambition, didactic moralizing, intellectual incoherence and the adolescent assumption that the past does not exist and the present needs only your guiding hand to create a glorious future" ("Saint Hillary," *New York Times Magazine*, May 23, 1993, pp. 22, 24). Seth Mandel, writing for *Commentary* (April 14, 2015) explains that Hillary Clinton achieves her fine art of gibberish "by diluting the English language until there are no more words, just empty sounds, hand gestures, and facial expressions" ("Clintonian Gibberish: The New Language of American Politics").

When President Obama refers to the legalization of same-sex marriage as the right to marry the person you love, his words seem to be appealing. After all, love and marriage go together "like a horse and carriage". If the listener is swept away by the sweet conjunction of love and marriage, he may forget what Obama's statement excludes, namely, the consent of the other, marital status, age, absence of blood relationship, willingness to carry out the responsibilities that is intrinsic to marriage. Being charmed by the sound of words, but failing to grasp their meaning, is the ideal subject for the master of gibberish.

Similarly, when Bernie Sanders boasts that he wants to remove all restrictions from abortion, his assertions may appear to be welcoming a courageous expansion of freedom. But to the thinking person, there are many factors that should restrict freedom. Even those who advocate abortion want some restrictions to be preserved, such as requiring the consent of the woman, ensuring that the abortionist is qualified and capable, and that health considerations are respected. No restrictions at all makes the woman vulnerable, allows the doctor to be irresponsible, and opens the way sheer mayhem.

Listening to a speaker must be more than an aesthetic experience. The speaker's voice and his words may be melodious and captivating, but they should not divert the listener from their meaning. The fine art of gibberish, is also the demagogue's instrument of deception.

DISHONESTY

An organization called the Canadian Centre for Bio-Ethical Reform has been sending out envelopes containing flyers depicting an aborted fetus. The intent is to remove the abortion discussion out of the abstract and inform people of what actually happens, typically, when an unborn child is aborted. At least one person is reported to have been offended by the picture and some postal workers refuse to deliver it, stating that the material is too graphic.

Being offended these days has become a discussion stopper. Some people believe that they have a right to go through life without ever being offended. Therefore, being offended is deemed to be so harmful to their psyche that any form of debate is simply out of the question. It is akin to being knocked out. Being offended, however, is often used as a tactic to avoid dialogue. In these instances it is more political than personal, more ideological than injurious. As far as images being "graphic", this seems to be an effective selling point for the motion picture industry.

People do not claim to be offended when they view graphic images in newspapers or magazines that show the deadly aftermath of hurricanes, tornados, or tsunamis. Nor are motorists who are charged with reckless driving offended when shown pictures of pedestrians killed by drunk drivers. Here the purpose is to enlighten and not to offend. It often happens, nonetheless, that people respond to an event with the wrong emotion, such as finding pleasure in someone else's pain. Sadism is not unknown.

A spokesperson for the Centre was interviewed on the radio recently (August 7, 2015). The interviewer did not see any educational value in the flyers. He made the rather dubious assertion that since a 7-year-old child may have an unwanted pregnancy, it is more than obvious that we need abortion across the board. To her credit, the Centre's representative kept her cool and tried to return the discussion to education (what really happens in an abortion), human rights (all human beings have the right to live), and how violence is not a solution to personal problems (there are many agencies that can provide help).

No real discussion ever took place. The interviewer, rather than respond to these objectively based points, implied that since many of the people who worked for the Center had religious affiliations (or so he presumed), their position had no credibility. This gambit, of course, was prejudicial and unwarranted. He seemed more concerned about real pictures possibly offending people than the fact that tens of thousands of unborn children are killed every year.

While listening to the interview, I became infuriated. I do not think I would have remained as calm and collected as did the Centre's spokesperson. The thought came to me that his view on abortion was completely formed, not by reality, but by the Media for which political correctness is *de rigueur*. He ended the interview by reminding his audience that he occupied the polar opposite of his guests' position and expressed confidence that he was firmly on the side of the enlightened. I thought his view was the height of ignorance. He was, without realizing it, against human rights, against education, against the integrity of the family, against religion, and stubbornly opposed to dialogue. Was he a mental zombie? It was a good thing, I thought, that I was not the one who was interviewed.

I gradually calmed down and recalled a wise statement penned by Robert Louis Stevenson: "There is so much good in the worst of us, and so much bad in the best of us, that it behooves all of us not to talk about the rest of us." Here is a basis for dialogue. How can we touch, with the good that we have, the common good that exists in all of us so that a respectful dialogue can commence? "Dialogue" is a wonderful term and meant a great deal to the ancient Greeks. It had reference to speaking "across" the "logos" or the knowable aspect of reality to which we all have a common relationship. Reason is the universal capacity to uncover the intelligibility of things. We become better educated, more knowing when we dialogue with each other and share each other's insights into the order of reality.

Martin Buber held dialogue in this form very highly. For the author of *I-Thou*, dialogue was a prerequisite for any authentic relationship between persons as well as between man and God. Such "true dialogue" is based on openness, honesty, and mutual commitment. It is a profoundly sad reality today that the "pro-life" and the "pro-choice" camps remain two monologues in search of dialogue. The former, however, does not shrink from inquiry; the latter does. This is an important point. Dialogue continues to be a neglected and unused form of discussion. We all share the same reality, but not all of us are looking in the same direction.

In his 1990 encyclical, *Redemptoris Missio,* John Paul II exhorted those engaged in dialogue to "be open to understanding those of the other party without pretense or close-mindedness, but with truth, humility and frankness, knowing that dialogue can enrich each side." For the now canonized saint, dialogue is not simply a tactic, but a pathway to a shared communion in truth. Those who take dialogue seriously, it should be emphasized, must take it not as an end in itself, but must subordinate toward the realization of a truth that embraces both parties. This is an ideal that needs to be applied to the life issues. Where there is no genuine dialogue, division and confusion perdure.

NEWSPEAK

Things change. **I change, as do others.** And the times change. Given this kaleidoscope of multifarious changes, it is hard to know whether things are getting better or worse. Is the world going crazy, or am I, as the years roll on, becoming more critical? Are my students getting smarter or are they conforming more and more to the *Zeitgeist*? Is social progress inevitable? Or does social regress remain a possibility?

Amidst all these simultaneous changes there is one thing that surely remains constant, namely the principle of contradiction. When we examine how language is being used these days, it is only too clear that contradictions abound. There is a clear contradiction between what is proposed and what is practiced. This is symptomatic of a deeper problem on the level of a significant misreading of reality.

When I began teaching, many moons ago, language was not an issue. It was a time before political correctness set in. Words meant something definable and acceptable. *Webster's Dictionary* was an unquestioned authority. Students did not reprimand me for using words that are now deemed politically insensitive. In more recent years, students have chided me (as well as other teachers) for using such words as "God," "truth," "girl," "moral," "chastity," and even the word "better". If the latter term seems far-fetched, it should be noted that the director of the Van Cliburn piano competition told the *New York Times* that "We must stamp out the concept of 'better'." In the minds of my latter-day students, a new sensitivity had arrived in which people were much kinder to minorities and less willing to make moral judgments. These politically correct students found a new morality that entitled them to an air of superiority and permission to criticize their elders. The SNAG had burst upon the scene (Sensitive New Age Guy).

Yet, a different snag had come into view. While mercy was doled out in abundance to the allegedly oppressed, no such mercy was shown to the alleged oppressors. Pro-life people became "anti-choice". Anyone who criticized homosexual activities was "homophobic". Critics of sex outside of marriage were labeled "uptight". Defenders of traditional marriage had to bear the brunt of being called "bigoted". Married couples who had more than two children were branded as "socially irresponsible". In addition, obscene words became standard fare on TV and in motion pictures. It was hard not to notice that the verbal revolution was decidedly one-sided.

The trend reached a point of utter silliness when "French doors," "Dutch treat," "Indian Summer," "Christmas parties," "penmanship," "niggardly," and "mankind" were added to the growing list of censorious terms. At the same time, lap dancing, pornography, coarse language and telephone sex became trendy. The fact that the teacher became muzzled was humorously represented by Gary Trudeau in his satire of what little is safe to say in a commencement speech: "A faculty panel of deconstructionists have reconfigured the rhetorical components within a post-structuralist framework, so as to expunge any offensive elements of Western rationalism and linear logic". All the commencement speaker had left to say to the graduates was "Thank you and good luck". James Finn Garner, in his satire on bedtime stories depicts the wolf in *The Three Little Pigs* as a "carnivorous, imperialistic oppressor". Little Red Riding Hood's grandmother "was not sick, but was rather in full physical and mental health and was fully capable of taking care of herself as a mature adult." Goldilocks was "a biologist who specialized in anthropomorphic bears". And Rumpelstiltskin was not a dwarf, but "a man of nonstandard height".

This evident contradiction between ultra-sensitivity on the one hand and extreme callousness on the other, can be explained as an extension of the Marxist philosophy that one class of people (the capitalists, the elite, or the conservatives) are all bad, while another class (the proletariat, the common people, or the liberals) are all good. The former group is characterized as the "oppressors" while the latter group is characterized as the "oppressed". Thus, the pro-life people are all oppressive while the pro-abortionists are all oppressed. This facile division, appealing as it may be for some people, is founded on nothing more than sheer prejudice. Although it aims at a new tolerance, it becomes exceedingly intolerant to anyone who does not accept the arbitrary canons of political correctness. We should watch our language, by all means, but in the sense that we realistically express what we want to say in terms that are appropriate for the occasion. When we refer to a Christmas Party, we should describe it for what it is rather than being unnecessarily watchful that the expression might offend someone who pays more attention to the political aspect of the phrase rather than to its realistic meaning. We can all share reality; not all of us can share that truncated reality known as political correctness.

The Christian is called to rise above such gratuitous distinctions and announce to the world that God created all of us equal and endowed each one of us with an intrinsic dignity. Our language, therefore, should be universally respectful. We are neighbors and owe each other a debt of kindness. In contrast, the politically correct brigade attempts to transform a universal language into an ideology for a few, thereby initiating a culture war. George Orwell referred to this truncated language as "Newspeak". Language should unite us, not divide us. Great literature reminds us that language at its very best, expresses reality in ways that are informative, artistic, and memorable.

NOVELTY

A **prominent Canadian bishop**, some time ago, shared with me his frustrations with the press, a problem that was most certainly not peculiar to him. Saint John Paul II's long expected encyclical, *Veritatis Splendor* had appeared in 1993. This document addressed "fundamentals of the Church's moral teaching" and was considered as one of the major events of John Paul's pontificate. My episcopal associate, who was relatively new to his post, told me that he cloistered himself for a week in order to read and digest thoroughly this encyclical before providing the press with an accurate summation. Alas, when the bishop was ready, the press was not interested in what he had to say since it was now stale and no longer news. The press, given its penchant for "what's happening right now," is more willing to accept reports that are hastily read and inaccurately delivered, than in those that are properly understood and reliably expressed.

At the heart of the encyclical was a reasoned discussion of the need to harmonize freedom with truth, something not only essential for one's personal moral life, but also for a healthy democracy. Detached from truth, freedom quickly degenerates into chaos. Nonetheless, the press, in some instances, both in Great Britain and in America, derided *Veritatis Splendor* as the effort of one pope imposing his own brand of thinking on the rest of the world. Being wrong does not require much time or effort; being right is an entirely different matter. The question prevails: can the press be a reliable conduit of information concerning matters, such as Vatican encyclicals, that are complex and controversial?

Bishop Fulton J. Sheen recounts an experience he had while he was still a student at the University of Louvain in which he encountered a popular philosopher who was more interested in what is new than in what is enduring. Samuel Alexander's book, *Space, Time, and Deity*, had created somewhat of a sensation. The author had proposed a novel view of God as the deification of time and space. Sheen, who, at that time, was working his thesis, *God and Intelligence in the Modern World*, asked him if he would be interested in reading the philosophy of Thomas Aquinas. Alexander's response was perfectly in sync with the climate of his time: "No, I would not be interested because you become known in this world not through Truth, but through novelty, and my doctrine is novel."

Samuel Alexander's views were novel in 1922. He had his moment of fame. But his contribution has failed the test of time. He is no longer novel, and no longer in the public consciousness. Both Aquinas and Sheen continue to be both important and relevant. Truth is eternal; novelty is ephemeral. The press is for today, but not for tomorrow. When C. S. Lewis remarked that "All that is not eternal is eternally out of date," he did not have in mind that something novel could be up-to-date for a brief moment. To be novel is to be eternally out of date because novelty does not belong to the continuing stream of time. It is a deviation, a diversion, a distraction.

Truth, on the other hand, is eternal and does not belong to the fluctuating world of fashion, trend, or pop culture. All that participates in Truth, participates in Eternity. *Veritatis Splendor* will continue to be relevant a hundred years from now. The romance with novelty will surely lead to a quick divorce.

The difference between the press and the Church may be likened to the difference between stimulation and inspiration. The news is stimulating. Hence, its lurid accounts of crimes, horrors, and tragedies. The news feasts on things that are sensational. The sensational is a stimulus, but as with the case of other stimuli, it is short-lived and requires repeated daily injections. Drugs are stimulating, but also evanescent. We cannot live by stimulation alone.

The Church is not in the business of stimulating people. She is, rather, in the art of inspiring its members. "A thing of beauty is a joy forever," wrote the poet, John Keats. Truth, like beauty, is also forever. Inspiration endures. It is more like a steady beacon than a momentary spark. Inspiration humanizes us, carries us beyond the moment. It lifts us above the dreary day-to-day quality of life. When the impressionist, Auguste Renoir, who had severe arthritis in his hands, was asked why he continues to paint since it brings him so much pain. He responded by saying that his pain is momentary, whereas his paintings will last. Things that inspire rise above the plane of self-indulgence.

The Church is larger than the world. Yet the world is constantly attempting to draw the Church into itself, to explain or criticize the Church in terms of its own narrow principles, which, themselves, are ever changing. The daily news is hardly fit to grasp and convey thought that goes well beyond itself. We get a sense of the breadth and depth of the Church's moral teaching in reading Saint John Paul II's Introduction to *Veritatis Splendor*: "The specific purpose of the present encyclical is this: to set forth, with regard to the problems being discussed, the principles of a moral teaching based upon Sacred Scripture and the living Apostolic Tradition, and at the same time to shed light on the presuppositions and consequences of the dissent which that teaching has met." This offers a challenge, broad and wide in scope, that exceeds the capacities of the daily press.

COWARDICE

Climate change, President Barack Obama assures us, "can no longer be denied." He is certainly on safe ground here since no one over the past few hundred years would deny it. It is an indisputable fact like saying that history is about the past, and we can no longer deny it. But why the bravado? "It can't be edited out," he goes on to say, "It can't be omitted from the conversation. And action can no longer be delayed." The President is presenting on obviosity as if it were an insight.

A high school student would be puzzled by this since he would know from his rudimentary science courses that planet earth and climate change have been inseparably intertwined from the very beginning. He would know, if he were attentive to his reading assignments, that the earth was formed around 4.54 billion years ago by accretion from the solar nebula. Volcanic outgassing may have been key factors in producing the ocean and a primordial atmosphere which at that time contained almost no oxygen. Much of the earth was molten because of frequent collisions with other celestial bodies. Changes were dramatic, violent, and constant. The first forms of life appeared between 3.8 and 3.5 billion years ago. Photosynthetic life appeared approximately 2 billion years ago providing the atmosphere with oxygen. Climate changes have been either providential or calamitous to the innumerable species of life that emerged over eons of time. More than 99% of all species—roughly five billion in number—have become extinct. The number of current species that inhabit the planet range from 10 to 14 million, of which, about 1.2 million have been documented and more than 86% have yet to be described and catalogued.

Meteorological and geological changes have been constantly occurring on Earth since the time of its formation. These changes combined with biological changes once life appeared on the scene. The biosphere affects the atmosphere and other abiotic conditions such as the ozone layer. In sum, these changes are stupendous, prodigious, and certainly undeniable.

Now the point here is not to criticize the president for what he said, but for other, and even more important things, that he could have said but chose not to say. For example, can we imagine Obama proclaiming the following: "The humanity of the fetus can no longer be denied. It can't be edited out. It can't be omitted from the conversation. And action can no longer be delayed." If he dared say such a thing he would be on equally firm ground with the reality of climate change, but he would not be in accord with political correctness. Certain truth, then, should not fall victim to politics, but, if they are to be proclaimed, should stand on the strength of courage.

The President has talked wistfully about how sad it would be if American children of the future could not enjoy the pristine natural beauty of the great national parks. But it seems to escape his attention that in order to be spectator to such beauty, one must be alive. The millions of aborted children will never have the opportunity to enjoy such splendors. Again, this is not to criticize the president for allocating many millions of dollars to improving the environments of America's national parks, but to point out his refusal to proclaim other important truths and the inconsistencies involved in the truths he chooses to proclaim.

Paul Tillich makes an important distinction between "world" and "environment". As human beings, he states in *Morality and Beyond*, "Having a world is more than having an environment. Of course, man, like any other being has an environment; but in contrast to the higher animals, he is not bound to it. He can transcend it in any direction, in imagination, thought and action." Animals are bound to their environment and this helps to explain that environmental changes have claimed more than 99% of all species. But man lives is a world of freedom within which he is able to become a truly unique person. Just as the state exists for man, and not vice versa, the environment exists for man and not the other way around.

Al Gore gave the wrong priority to the environment in his 1992 book, *Earth in the Balance* when he declared that "We must make the rescue of the environment the central organizing principle for civilization." But the environment cannot be central and human beings peripheral. As Saint John Paul II has insisted time and again, "the center of the social order is man." It is preposterous in the strictest sense to put the environment first and man second (*prae + posterious* means putting first that which should come second). Man needs a "world" (*cosmos*, as the ancient Greeks called it) and the liberty it implies, in order to realize his potential as a unique personality. He was not made to sub-serve but to care for his environment.

An excessive concern for the environment can be accompanied by a diminishing concern for the rights of man. A lack of regard for the nature and rights of the unborn together with a similar lack of regard for other moral verities such as personal liberty, marriage, and religion can inhibit personal growth. Courage is needed in order to proclaim fundamental truths about man that happen to be politically incorrect. Alexander Solzhenitsyn's famous words delivered at Harvard in 1978 continue to ring true: "A decline in courage may be the most striking feature that an outside observer notices in the West today. The Western world has lost its civic courage . . . Such a decline in courage is particularly noticeable among the ruling and intellectual elite, causing an impression of a loss of courage by the entire society."

CHAPTER FOUR
THE DEATH OF EDUCATION

BLINDNESS

C. S. Lewis, in *Mere Christianity,* asserts that "Good people know about both good and evil: bad people do not know about either." This is a bold statement. In today's world it would be dismissed not only as politically incorrect, but as both judgmental as well as offensive. Nonetheless, it is a matter of common sense. Good people know what good is. Therefore, since evil is a privation of good, they also know something about evil. But bad men, because they do not know what good is, cannot know what evil is. When we are awake, we know both what being awake is as well as what being asleep is. But while we are asleep, we know neither.

In *I Corinthians*, II, 15, St. Paul states, "But he who is spiritual judges all things, yet he himself is *rightly* judged by no one" (New King James version). In Matthew 6, 23 and in Luke 11, 34, we are told that "If the eye is worthless, your whole body is in darkness." Lewis's assertion is well supported by Scripture. Sixth century philosopher, Boethius sharply criticized those "who slay the rich and powerful harvest of Reason with the barren thorns of Passion. They habituate men to their sickness of mind instead of curing them." It is an old story. And it continues to be played out.

Education is firmly on the side of enlightenment. But education has run into a major problem in today's world in which it is considered unforgivable to make anyone feel uncomfortable. And some truths do precisely that. But education is supposed to be enlightening, not necessarily comforting. It begins with the mind, not with feelings. But if his mind is in darkness, then the will has lost its reliable guide and the whole person is plunged into darkness.

I was led to think about these things after reading an account by a certain Lia Mills who was thrown out of her classroom because she thought that education began with open-minded reasoning rather than by clinging to a closed-minded ideology. During a class discussion on the proper use of language, her professor stated that she is "always careful to refer to those who oppose abortion as 'anti-choice', since they stand in opposition to a woman's right to choose."

Miss Mills ventured to express a more reasonable opinion. "They are not 'anti-choice', she said and proceeded to defend her claim by pointing out that we would not say that every person who opposes murder or rape is 'anti-choice'. To bolster her argument she went on to say that those who oppose abortion are not 'anti-choice' since they support most choices, "so long as the choice doesn't interfere with the rights of another human being."

This seemingly mild and sensible line of reasoning, incorporating indisputable facts, opened the floodgates to hostility and invective. Miss Mills was eventually ousted from the class. She had crossed the line and made other students feel uncomfortable. She was told to censor herself in order to avoid making other people feel uncomfortable in the future. This meant that she should keep her "offensive, discriminatory beliefs" to herself. In addition, she was obliged to make an apology to the class. Her apology, however, was criticized, dissected and subsequently deemed "insensitive and insincere".

Lia Mills remains a stouthearted defender of reason. Her experience with her intolerant classmates only strengthened her resolve to employ reason in the defense of unborn life. She did not find the unreasonableness, intolerance, and hostility of her classmates to be an inducement to join the unthinking crowd. Her experience, one hopes, will open the eyes of the many people she addresses in the many pro-life talks she gives throughout North America. We might say, with C. S. Lewis, that she is a good person who know something about both good and evil.

In his 1879 encyclical on Christian philosophy, *Aeterni Patris*, Pope Leo XIII reminded his flock and the rest of the world, that "since it is in the very nature of man to follow the guide of reason in his actions, if his intellect sins at all his will soon follows; and thus it happens that false opinions, whose seat is in the understanding, influence human actions and pervert them." Pope Leo was not thinking about abortion when he penned these words. Nonetheless, they apply to the present abortion discussion very well. When the eye does not see, the will is also in darkness. When the nature of the unborn human being is not seen for what it is, all sorts of perversions follow.

C. S. Lewis, together with St. Paul, St. Matthew, St. Luke, Boethius, Pope Leo XIII, and, yes, Lia Mills, make a formidable tandem in defense of reason, education, and the pro-life cause. I would imagine that even Pope Leo XIII, had been enrolled in Lia Mills' feminist class, would have been asked to leave. The pontiff was a great champion of philosophy, especially the philosophy of St. Thomas Aquinas. In his aforementioned encyclical he stated that Aquinas "victoriously combated the errors of former times, and supplied invincible arms to put those to rout which might in after-times spring up."

Philosophy is never out of season. Because it is both a universal and timeless human faculty, it rises above party interests and passing fads. Pro-life people are not anti-choice. Their adversaries, however, are anti-reason.

The Good Shepard discriminates between sheep and goats.

DISCRIMINATION

On May 17, 2016, the Halton Catholic District School Board (Ontario) rejected, by a 4-3 vote, an updated disciplinary policy intended to make their schools "safer" and more "inclusive" for lesbians, gays, bisexuals, and transgendered persons (LGBT). The vote has sparked a storm of outrage.

In defense of the vote, Jane Michael, board chair reminded people that "The church recognizes the dignity of all persons and neither defines nor catalogues them according to their sexual orientation." In other words, all groups are covered, whether they are left-handed, portly, anorexic, spectacled, slow-footed, vegans, witches or warlocks. There is no need to establish a special policy to protect any of these groups. They are all protected under the umbrella of Catholic teaching. To offer special treatment for one group over all the others could be viewed as discriminatory. Passing a special law that punishes anyone who laughs at stutterers will not make them any safer since they are already protected as human beings.

One of the provisions in the defeated policy states that evidence of "homophobia" can result in suspension from school. This word, of recent coinage, is an ideological invention to serve as a tool for discrediting anyone who dares to argue against homosexual sexual relations. It prevents any rational discussion by accusing anyone who disapproves of homosexual activities as being sick, which is what the suffix "phobia" implies.

In 1973, the American Psychiatric Association voted to dissociate homosexuality from any kind of sickness. While the term "heterophobia" is not widely used, heterosexuals are continuously labelled "homophobic" merely because they, as well as many who are homosexually inclined, see something wrong with homosexual sexual activity. The AIDS phenomenon offers dramatic evidence that certain homosexual acts are disordered. Is a school policy needed in order to protect heterosexuals from being maligned as "homophobic"? This is a matter that is never discussed.

In 1992, the National Association for Research & Therapy for Homosexuality (a non-religious organization) was founded because the American Psychiatric Association's 1973 decision had made it politically incorrect even to discuss the need for any dialogue concerning the normalcy of the homosexual condition. In an article entitled, "In Defense of an Honest Dialogue," Benjamin Kaufman, one of NARTH's founders, made the comment that the 1973 decision "had totally stifled the scientific inquiry that would be necessary to stimulate a discussion" about homosexuality. As scientific research was either censored or ignored, the so-called normalcy of homosexuality became acceptable. Buzz words replaced scientific knowledge. Education was forced to take a back seat.

Moreover, what does "homophobia" really mean? When we examine the word, it appears to refer to an unnatural fear of anything that is the same. Presumably, this would include a fear of homonyms, homogenized milk, and all homologues. Should a student at a Catholic school be suspended for continuingly refusing to drink homogenized milk? Being accused of "homophobia" does not make one sick, but it calls into question the integrity of the accuser.

Many who lambasted the policy claimed that it left LGBT students unsafe. This claim, doubtless to say, accords a power to a policy that a policy simply does not have. It is not the policy that makes students safe, but proper behavior, which is exactly what Catholic education attempts to inculcate. This is not to argue against policies, but to point out that they are often violated and the main objective of a Catholic education is to inspire students to behave properly. The Commandment to love one's neighbor is a stronger mandate than whatever policy a School Board may or may not approved. It is ironic that critics will put more trust in a policy composed by members of a School Board than in a Commandments issued by God.

Also, since the term "homophobia" is an artificial concoction, it is, not surprisingly, used recklessly. It is used to castigate anyone who disapproves of homosexual sexual acts. Now there is good reason for such disapproval, just as there are good reasons to disapprove of heterosexual acts of an adulterous nature. As an example of this reckless use of the term, The Social Research at the University of Saskatoon has publicized its conclusion that "Thousands Die Each Year As A Result of Homophobia" (March 20, 2004). This dubious study was undertaken through Gay & Lesbian Health

Services of Saskatoon.   Executive Director, Gens Hellquist, concludes that "I think it is safe to say that the 5,500 deaths each year from homophobia are only the tip of the iceberg." As science and philosophy are devalued, ideology reigns unchecked.

The irony of the Halton School Board's vote is that it protects Catholics from the possibility of being suspended from Catholic schools for being Catholic.   The Church teaches that, on the basis of the Natural Law, homosexual acts are intrinsically disordered. This teaching, it should be noted, is not restricted to homosexuals, but to heterosexuals who partake of disordered sexual acts.   The Church is inclusive insofar as it includes everyone.   But it is not inclusive, along with every organization that came into existence, with regard to behavior.   Secular schools explicitly condemn bullying, for example.   Yet the secular world seems intolerant of a Catholic position that denounces certain sexual activities that are not only harmful, but often lead to death.

Thus, it is the Catholic school that is truly inclusive and protective. And she offers these benefits to everyone.   Her secular opponents are not as inclusive since they do not want to include real Catholics, and, perhaps unwittingly, seek to expose students to real harm.   It is a topsy-turvy world we live in at the moment.   Catholic School Board members should have the courage of their Catholic convictions and remove arbitrary roadblocks that prevent them from doing their work, which is also God's work.

INCONSISTENCY

The great moral maxim, "Do unto others as you would have them do unto you," from an historical perspective, is perhaps the most highly respected of all moral maxims. It did not originate with Christianity, as some may believe, but was a component of Greek philosophy, Judaism, Confucianism, Zoroastrianism, Buddhism, Hinduism, and Taoism. Its equally binding corollary is "Do not do unto others what you would not have them do unto you." Underlying this honored principal is the notion of human equality. No person should arrogate to himself the right to do something to another person that he would not have that person do to him. Religion reinforces this notion since all human beings are created by the same God, no one person being more human than any other.

Abraham Lincoln exemplified the Golden Rule when he remarked: "As I would not be a slave, so I would not be a master." In making this enunciation, America's sixteenth president was also underscoring his belief in democracy. Both slavery and the ownership of a person are clearly incompatible with the Gold Rule. So, too, is political despotism.

Bassanio, in Shakespeare's *The Merchant of Venice*, demonstrated wisdom when he stated that "All that glitters is not gold." Glitter made him suspicious. He would have no reason, however, to be suspicious about the proposition "All that is gold glitters." The Golden Rule, being of a golden kind, does glitter, as does any moral truth. Saint John Paul II used the expression "Splendor of Truth" as the title of the encyclical in which he devoted his most concerted attention to moral principles. Gold should glitter, and truth should radiate a certain splendor. A serious moral problem arises when their shine and splendor, respectively, are not perceived as such.

The word "glitterati," refers to glamourous people who attend fashionable events. It is a hybrid of "glitter" and "literati" and is usually used pejoratively, although in a sophisticated way, to describe people who are all show and little substance. The glitterati, in other words, are not gold. They do not personify the "gold" of the Golden Rule. They presume to be superior to others the way the ancient sophists presumed to be wise.

Hollie McKay, writing for FoxNews.com claims that in order to be pro-life, one must "go against the grain of the glitterati". It is hardly a secret, she states, concerning abortion, that "the majority of Hollywood stars are strong advocates of a woman's right to choose". Advocates of abortion, however, are not ambassadors of the Golden Rule. Glitter alone does not serve the real character needs of the denizens of Tinsel Town. The Greek playwright, Aeschylus said it well long ago: "Ah, lives of men! When prosperous they glitter – Like a fair picture; when misfortune comes – A wet sponge at one blow has blurred the painting."

Just as Abraham Lincoln would neither be a slave nor a master, so, too, no one should want to be a killer or be killed. Abortion, therefore, has removed the glitter from the Golden Rule. The abortionist does not view the unborn in an egalitarian spirit. He does not see the child in the womb as another human being who, because of his common humanity, stands against being executed. He sees his victim not as a neighbor but as a complete stranger.

Philosopher/Theologian Paul Tillich, in his thoughtful book, *Love, Power, Justice*, argues that "The absolutely strange cannot enter into communion. But the estranged is striving for reunion." By making the unborn a completely "strange" entity, its communion with the mother is greatly attenuated. The unborn, in Tillich's language, has become "estranged," as have so many others who are not perceived to exist within the ambit of the Golden Rule. Therefore, Tillich can say that love is "the reunion of the estranged". Love invites the estranged, the abandoned, and the despised back into the equality that the Golden Rule demands.

By practicing the Golden Rule, a woman can say, "Since I am glad that I was not aborted by my mother, I cannot abort my own child. I was once a child in the womb. It is precisely because I rejoice in not having been aborted that I cannot deprive my own child in the womb of its opportunity for a fuller life. The Golden Rule unites me with my child and I would not do to that other what I would not want to have been done to me."

The Golden Rule has lost much of its glitter, which is to say, its compelling attractiveness. We still have glitter, but it is the glitter than has been separated from gold. The Golden Rule, therefore, has been replaced by the "Glitter Rule": Do unto others what you would not want them to do unto you. Glitter can be seductive, but it can never serve as a guide for loving human relationships.

Finally, if we understand "gold" in its deeper sense as something that does not necessarily glitter, but is worthwhile and highly to be prized, we can agree with J.R.R. Tolkien who, in *The Fellowship of the Ring*, offers us the following sample of his poetic imagination:

> All that is gold does not glitter,
> Not all those who wander are lost;
> The old that is strong does not wither,
> Deep roots are not reached by the frost.

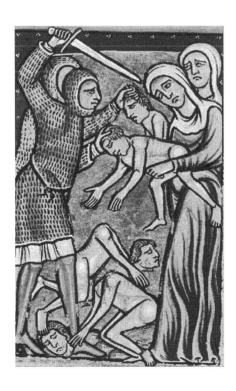

DEMAGOGUERY

The issue of whether America is still a great society has come up again and again during the presidential campaigns. Does the word "great" accurately characterize the present culture that is the United States?

In order to deal with this question, the first thing one must do is to establish the criteria for greatness. There are two that are most worthy of discussion: 1) how society treats its weakest members; 2) the civility of discourse among its strongest members.

"A nation's greatness," stated Mahatma Ghandi, "is measured by how it treats its weakest members." Author Pearl S. Buck echoed this sentiment when she declared that "the test of a civilization is the way that it cares for is helpless members." Ancient Sparta took the opposite approach which brought about its total collapse as a nation. It is remembered as a society that gambled on military strength and the survival of the fittest, only to self-destruct. The same can be said of the Roman Empire. Social Darwinism has proven to be counter-evolutionary. Human beings survive and prosper because of love, not strength.

In his last speech, former vice-president, Hubert H. Humphrey, stated the matter more pointedly: ". . . the moral test of government is how that government treats those who are in the dawn of life, the children; those who are in the twilight of life, the elderly; those who are in the shadows of life, the sick, the needy and the handicapped."

United States President Jimmy Carter affirmed what Humphrey stated when he commented that "The measure of a society is found in how they [sic] treat their weakest and most helpless citizens." Finally, from a Catholic perspective, Cardinal Roger Mahoney stated that "Any society, any nation, is judged on the basis of how it treats its weakest members – the last, the least, the littlest." And societies are, indeed, judged.

In present day America, no one has a right to life for the first nine months of his existence. Presidential candidate Bernie Sanders wants "no restrictions" placed on abortion" (which, logically, would allow forcing certain women to have abortions). Hillary Clinton declares that the "unborn person" has no rights whatsoever. At the other end of the spectrum, organizations such as "Compassion and Choice" are relentless in their promotion of euthanasia for the elderly or anyone who wants to end his life. Life at the edges of life is now greatly imperiled. Should only the strong inherit the earth?

The present picture in which the strongest survive and the weakest are left unprotected looks more like a heartless society that a great one. It has the Darwinian character of the survival of the fittest and not an abiding concern for the weakest.

Civil discourse, especially among the well-educated, is currently impoverished, often descending to the level of insult and abuse. Martin Buber once remarked that the inability to "carry on authentic dialogue with one another is the most acute symptom of the pathology of our time." The proper use of words, vital for meaningful communication appears to be vanishing from society. Words are replaced by arbitrary constructs that serve ideological purposes.

To speak about abortion, for example, as an instance of "domestic violence," which it is, would provoke anger and outrage among pro-choice advocates. The notion of "dying with dignity," in the push for euthanasia, is a pure construct and disregards the more important mandate of "living with dignity". People can no longer agree on the meaning of words. "Marriage," "morality," "male," "female," "virtue," are twisted out of shape. Hence, communication, especially on critical moral issues, becomes problematic if not impossible.

The argument that America has descended into barbarism is not without merit. The ancient Greeks ridiculed people who spoke in alien languages. They believed that such people were merely babbling incoherently. The word "barbarism" was coined to mimic the meaningless sound of "bar-bar". Those who uttered such sounds were called "barbarians".

Rémi Brague, a French Professor of Religious philosophy, believes that the West has fallen into barbarism because of its inability to communicate. "Civilization means conversation," he states, and without communication, violence follows." A nation cannot work effectively towards the elimination of violence if it cannot use meaningful verbal expression to solve its problems.

The blindly accepted myth of progress has led to a rejection of the past. This rejection, however, means that we no longer communicate with the past. By the same token, future generations, beguiled by their own sense of superiority, will reject the accomplishments of the present generation. They may think that the wisdom of the past is nothing more than a reiteration of "bar-bar". Barbarism can also be understood as severing the connection between those who are dead and those who are yet to be born. It is intellectually isolationistic and deprives itself of nourishment from the triumphs of the past and altruistic spirit that is mindful of the future. The net result is confusion, as in the Tower of Babel. When people can no longer speak to each other, they can no longer work together. Society, then, disintegrates. Violence becomes the desperate alternative to communication.

Is America a great society? Providing and enforcing laws that remove care from its weakest members, and being unable to communicate meaningfully on critical moral issues would seem to indicate that America is now closer to barbarism than it is to greatness.

Scott

Taney

Curtis

Blackmun

White

Obergefell

Kennedy

Hodges

Scalia

IDEOLOGY

The United States Supreme Court is so named not because it exemplifies consistent wisdom, but because there is no higher judiciary to which a claim can be appealed. This Court, over the years, has made some truly horrible decisions. And these decisions were not made because the Constitution was properly interpreted. The *Dred Scott* decision of 1857 denied citizenship to blacks. In dissent Justice Benjamin Robbins Curtis wrote: "[W]hen a strict interpretation of the Constitution, according to the fixed rules which govern the interpretation of laws, is abandoned and the theoretical opinions of individuals are allowed to control its meaning, we no longer have a Constitution; we are under the government of individual men, who for the time being have power to declare what the Constitution is, according to their own views of what it ought to mean."

The *Buck v. Bell* ruling in 1927 permitted forced sterilization. Justice Oliver Wendell Holmes, Jr. stated that "The principle that sustains compulsory vaccination is broad enough to cover cutting the Fallopian tubes. Three generations of imbeciles is enough." In *Roe v. Wade* (1973) Justice Harry A. Blackmun found, "implied in the penumbra," a constitutional right to abortion. In dissent, Byron White labeled his ruling an "exercise of raw judicial power".

And now, on June 25, 2015, in *Obergefell v. Hodges*, Justice Kennedy ruled that the Constitution provided same-sex couples the liberty to marry. In dissent Chief Justice John G. Roberts declared the "this Court is not a legislature. Whether same-sex marriage is a good idea should be of no concern to us. The people who ratified the Constitution authorized the courts to exercise 'neither force nor will but merely judgment'." Interesting, the Court offered little respect for the 1972 *Baker v. Nelson* case which declared that there is no constitutional right to homosexual marriage.

The present situation may be more dire and discouraging than even the period following the dreadful decision of 1857. Soon after that infamous ruling, President Abraham Lincoln stated, in his first inaugural address, that "if the policy of the government upon vital questions, affecting the whole people, is to be irrevocably fixed by decisions of the Supreme Court, the instant they are made . . . the people will have ceased to be their own rulers, having to that extent practically resigned their government into the hand of that eminent tribunal."

In response to the same-sex decision President Obama, unconcerned about eroding democracy and the raw judicial power of the Supreme Court, had this to say to the Press: "An entire country realized that love is love." That "love is love" is a tautology and not in insight that required the expertise of the Supreme Court to discover and enunciate. The central issue, of course, has nothing to do with love, but whether there is a provision in the Constitution to alter the time-honored definition of marriage so that it is no longer limited to a union between a man and a woman. The U.S. President would have been more on target had he said that the ruling proved that "democracy is not democracy".

This is what Justice Antonin Scalia had firmly in mind when, in dissent, he made the following statement: "And to allow the policy question of same-sex marriage to be considered and resolved by a select, patrician, highly unrepresentative panel of nine is to violate a principle even more fundamental than no taxation without representation . . . A system of government that makes the People subordinate to a committer of nine unelected lawyers does not deserve to be called a democracy."

Obergefell v. Hodges, like *Dred Scott*, may, in time, be reversed. But Barack Obama is no Abraham Lincoln. If it is to be reversed it would be under the watchful eye of a far different Chief of State, one who values that government "of the people, by the people, and for the people".

CHAPTER FIVE
THE DEATH OF DEMOCRACY

THE LOSS OF NATURE

The great mistake of our primal parents was their belief in moral autonomy. Consequently, they believed that they did not need the guidance of God in order to determine what is good and what is evil. Their disobedience itself, and consequent estrangement from their Maker, offered sufficient evidence that their ability to make moral judgments was defective. Their Original Sin was to put themselves first and reality second, a disorder of the first magnitude.

This same mistake is being played out in contemporary society. It is now commonly believed that we do not need an objective basis for determining what is good and what is evil; we can do that ourselves. As a result, the illusion of moral autonomy replaces the objective reality of the Natural Law. What should be regarded as an invitation to chaos, is popularly regarded as a strike for open-mindedness, tolerance, and freedom. Nonetheless, we do not "determine" or "cause" the nature of things; we discover them.

Pope Benedict was a minority voice in pleading that the Natural Law must be the foundation of democracy. This law would give people a common and unifying basis for distinguishing between both good and evil, as well as between right and wrong. Ancient Greece gave birth to democracy because it also gave birth to philosophy. Because there is an intelligible reality, any intelligent person can see the truth of things. Therefore, philosophy is possible. Because these truths (such as the value of life, liberty and the pursuit of happiness) can be embraced by society, people of good will can live together in peace and harmony. Therefore, democracy is possible.

In Walt Disney's *The Lady and the Tramp*, two animated cats pay respect to the rigorous continuity if the natural order of things. "We are Siamese if you please. We are Siamese if you don't please". Being a Siamese cat is a reality that is established independently of external opinion. Disney's oriental felines are not relativists in any sense. They know who they are and do not care what other people might think or say. They stubbornly "purr-sist," in being who they are. They illustrate the axiom that the order of naming should always conform to the order of being. But if the order of naming came first, then we would hear a different song: "We are Siamese if it pleases you, but if something else pleases you more, perhaps we are ragamuffins, Turkish angoras, Chantilly-tiffanies, or even panthers."

Without an objective basis for grasping the nature of things, chaos is inevitable: the nature of the unborn becomes indeterminable, marriage becomes uncertain, fatherhood becomes unnecessary, sex differences become fluid, and death becomes an option. If peace, as St. Augustine stated, is the "tranquility of order," this cherished, though elusive value cannot possibly be achieved in an atmosphere of total confusion.

Among the moral verities that are needed for democracy, according to the former pontiff, are "human dignity," "human life," "the institution of the family," and the "equity of the social order". These are essential verities, he reasoned, so that "skepticism and ethical relativism" do not "threaten to undermine the foundations of democracy and a just social order."

It is perhaps ironic that the Catholic Church can be a more realistic advocate for democracy than are many societies today that presume to be democratic. The Church continually teaches that it is far better, and certainly more democratic, for citizens to live and act in accordance with their natural inclinations than to have political leaders impose on them arbitrary and artificial standards. Democracy is not only a government of the people, but one that is grounded in nature.

THE ABANDONMENT OF THE CONSTITUTION

In his classic work, *Democracy in America*, Alexis de Tocqueville states that "In the United States the majority governs in the name of the people . . . This majority is principally composed of peaceable citizens, who, either by inclination or by interest, sincerely wish the welfare of their country." This is a beautiful statement. Yet, can we affirm these words about democracy in America in todays' climate? Is Lincoln's ideal of "that government of the people, by the people, and for the people," still operative? In fact, we may dare to ask, is it still desirable?

In his first inaugural address (1861), America's 16th president acknowledged that it is possible for the Supreme Court to render a "decision that may be erroneous in any given case". He therefore, warned against the kind of judicial activism that allows for such decisions, and the failure on the part of the people to take the initiative to overturn them. He then reminded those peaceable citizens of democracy of their democratic obligations. "The candid citizen," he stated, "must confess that if the policy of the government, upon vital questions, affecting the whole people, is to be irrevocably fixed by the decisions of the Supreme Court, the instant they are made, in ordinary litigation between parties, in personal actions, the people will have ceased to be their own rulers, having to that extent, practically resigned their government, into the hands of that eminent tribunal." The infamous *Dred Scott* decision was not far from Lincoln's mind. A judicial oligarchy is not a democracy. Lincoln wanted to impress this on the minds and hearts of his fellow citizens.

The late Justice Antonin Scalia echoed these words of President Lincoln in his dissent from *Obergefell v. Hodges* (2015), referring to its decision "as a naked judicial claim to legislative—indeed, super-legislative—power; a claim fundamentally at odds with our system of government. Except as limited by a constitutional prohibition agreed to by the People, the States are free to adopt whatever laws they like, even those that offend

101

the esteemed Justices' 'reasoned judgment.' A system of government that makes the People subordinate to a committee of nine unelected lawyers does not deserve to be called a democracy." Scalia's words are strong, but not without justification. Nor are his thoughts without precedent.

Senator John Danforth, in his book, *Faith and Politics: How the "Moral Values" Debate Divides America and How to Move Forward Together*, argues that "the values of society are best expressed by the legislative branch of government, not the judicial branch." He found clear evidence of judicial activism the *Griswold* case (1965): "In my opinion, the Supreme Court had invented a right to privacy, created out of thin air, and that was a violation of judicial restraint and encroachment into the province of legislature." *Griswold* served as a basis for the "raw judicial power" (Byron White in dissent) of *Roe v. Wade*. America was moving away from how Lincoln so eloquently described it: "This country, with its institutions, belongs to the people who inhabit it."

Justice John Roberts called the *Obergefell* decision "an act of will, not legal judgment." Justice Sam Alito condemned the decision as revealing "the deep and perhaps irremediable corruption of our legal culture's conception of constitutional interpretation." Justice Clarence Thomas saw it "at odds not only with the Constitution, but the principles upon which our Nation was built." It was as if the Court had formally repudiated the very reason for the American Revolution. But does America really want to abandon its democratic heritage and prefer to be ruled by a few?

The rule of law is not the rule of judges. The enactment of law belongs to the legislative branch of the government. When there is a gross usurpation of the law by the Court, steps must be taken to return lawmaking authority back to the legislature. There is much work to be done if democracy in America is to be recovered.

Michael Stokes Paulsen is Distinguished University Chair and Professor at the University of St. Thomas Law School. In the October 2015 issue of *First Things* he expresses his conviction that "*Obergefell* completes a stunning social transformation in the millennia-old institution of marriage and seeks to locate and entrench that transformation, however implausibly, in the U.S. Constitution." What this means bodes ill for all those who defend traditional marriage and regard sexual acts between same-sex partners as disordered. Being compelled by the government to act contrary to one's religious beliefs violates "freedom of religion". But it also, and more importantly, violates a person's right to live and act in accord with his conscience. Insisting on the naturalness of traditional marriage should not be a crime, certainly not in a democracy.

Not only has America lost its Constitution and is now under a judicial dictatorship, but persecution of people of religion, especially, of Catholics, has been given governmental approval. Justice Alito's words are not to be taken lightly: "If a bare majority of Justices [5-4] can invent a new right and impose that right on the rest of the country, the only real limit on what future majorities will be able to do is their own sense of what those with political power and cultural influence are willing to tolerate." The People, therefore, are left out.

THE BANISHMENT OF RELIGION

The decline of religion in North American society presents a series of problems that are significant threats to all its citizens. The first problem, which is the direct result of undermining the importance of God or even negating his existence, is the illusion that man is autonomous. Without a viable relationship with the Creator, man begins to think that he is not dependent on any other being than himself. He believes that he is self-sufficient and can create his own morality. With the decline in Christianity, in particular, the notion of suffering becomes bereft of meaning. The crucified Christ no longer affords salvific meaning to suffering human beings. Thirdly, the autonomous self, who finds his suffering to be an intolerable burden, seeks to end it through physician-assisted suicide or some form of euthanasia. Standing in the way of such "self-deliverance" is a tradition as old as Hippocrates, which states that physicians should neither kill nor harm. Thus, in order for physician-assisted suicide to become a legal option, society, including the institutions of law, medicine, and politics, must cooperate fully. A new morality is on the scene. This leads inevitably to the deadening of conscience, which is now clearly manifested in both America and Canada.

These problems are pointing to a contradictory notion of man as an *autonomous automaton*. He is currently being viewed no longer as a social being, a creature of God, or a *person* who combines individual uniqueness with social responsibilities, but as someone who is allegedly independent but at the same time operates without a conscience. President Obama's belief in *choice* but not in *conscience* attests to this contradictory view.

The late Rev. Richard Neuhaus, founder of *First Things*, has made the comment that "in most aspects of life [in Canada] Christianity has been not only disestablished but also banished". On February 6, 2015, the Supreme Court of Canada invalidated that country's criminal prohibitions against assisted suicide and euthanasia as applied to physician assisted death. By a nine to nothing count, the Court ruled the previous holding to be unconstitutional. The Court interpreted the Constitution's rights to "life, liberty and security of the person" in a novel way, as including the right to die. The Court so ruled because it regards the human being as an autonomous agent who reserves the option to live or to die. Thus, it included the right to die within the right to live.

Dr. Margaret A. Somerville, a leading ethicist in Canada who is a lawyer and professor in the Faculty of Medicine at Montreal's McGill University, explains that the Court's decision grants "a right to control of one's bodily integrity and a right to be free of suffering, or even the fear of suffering, in the future". This utopian concept is directly opposed to the realistic notion that human life is inseparable from suffering. It implies that the only way to rid suffering is through death. In this way, the autonomous concept of the human being signs his death warrant.

The Court required that informed consent be obtained for "doctor assisted suicide and euthanasia". Nonetheless, such consent is not valid unless reasonable alternatives are provided. An important alternative is palliative care. Yet only 16 to 20 percent of all Canadians who need palliative care have access to it. The Canadian Medical Association, proposed as one of the main advisors to the government, has expressly stated that non-availability of palliative care should not be a reason to refuse physician-assisted suicide. Conscience, as the etymology of the word indicates, means "with knowledge". To suppress knowledge is to suppress conscience. In this way, the alleged autonomous individual merges with the automaton who has been deprived of the exercise of his own conscience, and therefore, the expression of his own free will. A spokesperson for the Ontario College of Physicians and Surgeons recently remarked that physicians not willing to refer for abortions should "get out of family medicine". The same dismissal of conscience in the area of abortion is now being transferred to the field of euthanasia.

Doug Bandow, writing for *Forbes* magazine asks, in the title of his February 6, 2012 article, "Why Does President Obama Dislike Freedom Of Conscience?" He argues that "authoritarian liberalism" (as contradictory an expression as "autonomous automaton") prevails throughout the Obama administration. "Acting on faith must be punished," he concludes. Just as euthanasia removes suffering by removing the sufferer, a united nation can be achieved by suppressing the conscience of dissenters. Dissent, which used to be proof that one was an independent thinker, is now passé. Uniformity is currently *de rigueur*. Representative Joe Pitts has complained that "Without legal protection, we can certainly expect even more bureaucratic assaults on the conscience of medical workers" (*Washington Post*, February 18, 2011).

The right to conscience is a paramount importance for the medical profession. It allows members of the profession the freedom to refuse to perform practices they oppose on either moral or religious grounds. The American College of Obstetricians and Gynecology, however, has stated that abortion is a social value that outweighs any conscientious objection. A 2009 survey conducted by The Polling Company/WomanTrend reported that 87 percent of adults held that "it is important to make sure that healthcare professionals in America are not forced to participate in procedures and practices to which they have moral objections." The present bureaucratic disregard for conscientious objection is driving health professionals out of their chosen field. Many have asserted, "I would rather stop practicing medicine altogether than be forced to violate my conscience". Nonetheless, according to President Obama, "A country's conscience sometimes has to be triggered by some inconvenience."

Religion, especially the Catholic religion, recognizes three things that the secular world vehemently rejects: the primacy of God, the rightful place of man as created by God and called to love both himself and his neighbor, and the redemptive value of suffering. Secular society may believe that it is being progressive by denying each of these factors, but the truth is, that the attempt to force human beings into an impossible role, which combines an illusion with a humiliation, places man on the road to death, both spiritually as well as physically. It is a phenomenon akin to what C. S. Lewis had in mind when he wrote about "The Abolition of Man". It is also consistent with the searing conclusion that Henri De Lubac derives in *The Drama of Atheist Humanism*, namely, that "man cannot organise the world for himself without God; without God he can only organise the world against man. Exclusive humanism is inhuman humanism."

North American society would do well to assimilate some of the ideas that Saint John Paul II has propounded concerning "anthropological realism". In his encyclical, *Veritatis Splendor*, the former pontiff states that "At the heart of the moral life we thus find the principle of a 'rightful autonomy' of man, the person as subject of his actions." This "rightful autonomy," as he explains in great detail in *The Acting Person*, involves "*self-governance* and *self-possession*" and not the unrealistic autonomy of self-sufficiency and independence. Conscience, therefore, despite its subjectiveness, retains a measure of "intersubjectivity" for it is in conscience that a person unites the objectivity of truth with the duty to live that truth. "In each of his actions," John Paul writes, "the human person is eyewitness of the transition from the 'is' to the 'should,' – the transition from '*X* is truly good' to 'I should do *X*.'" Secular society, being skeptical about knowing truth, fails to understand the first dynamic of conscience. As a result, it has little respect for it. In failing to respect conscience, the secular world then fails to respect the integrity of the human person. The unhappy result is that it cannot steer its citizens in the direction of life, but only encourage them to accept the illusion that they are free, while obliging them to conform to a world that is accurately described as a Culture of Death. Instead of an anthropological realism which is true to man's nature, the secular world imposes on him the unrealistic and impossible

task of being, at the same time, both "pro-choice" and "anti-conscience". A revolt will surely follow, for man cannot live a contradiction for very long.

THE END OF BROTHERHOOD

S aint John Paul II made a claim in his international best-selling book, *Crossing the Threshold of Hope*, that may be startling to many, namely, that Original Sin, is, above all, an attempt "to abolish fatherhood". Upon reflection, this statement makes a great deal of sense. After all, Adam and Eve chose to reject God and side with the serpent. This initial act of disobedience, or Original Sin, has cast a shadow that has covered all of human history. For the former Holy Father, the notion that God is not a loving Father, but as a tyrant or oppressor, has led to a rebellion against Him as a slave would rebel against the master who kept him enslaved. Whether God is a loving Father or an oppressor is perhaps the most fundamental of all moral questions.

In addition to the attempt to abolish the Fatherhood of God, is the outright rejection of Him. This rejection has an immediate impact on society in that it also represents the rejection of all forms of fatherhood. Writing for the *American Psychologist*, authors Louise B. Silverstein, and Carl F. Auerbach assert that "the argument that fathers are essential is an attempt to re-instate male dominance by restoring the dominance of

the traditional nuclear family with its contrasting masculine and feminine gender roles" ("Deconstructing the Essential Father," June 1999). A concerted attempt has been underway in the last few decades to "deculture" paternity. Fatherhood is something bad.

The attempt to abolish Fatherhood is by no means restricted to academia. For example, on the cover flap of Philip Pullman best-seller, *The Golden Compass* (which was made into a popular move),

109

the author offers us a brief description of his theology: "My sympathies definitely lie with the tempter. The idea that sin, the Fall, was a good thing. If it had never happened we would still be puppets in the hands of the Creator." Moreover, as he continues to inform us, "I am all for the death of God." "My books are about killing God." "I am of the Devil's Party and I know it." For Pullman, the principal evil in *The Golden Compass* is called "the Authority".

As a direct consequence of the derogation and dismissal of fatherhood, additional weight has been placed on "brotherhood". The "rainbow coalition" and all groups that profess to be "inclusive" exemplify this transition. Yet, there cannot be any true brotherhood without fatherhood, just as there cannot be offspring without parents.

David Blankenhorn has provided compelling evidence in his critical study, *Fatherless America: Confronting Our Most Urgent Social Problem*, that fatherlessness is the most harmful trend of the current generation: the leading cause of the declining well-being of children; the engine driving our most critical social problems, from crime to adolescent pregnancy to child sexual abuse to domestic violence against women. Such warnings, however, go largely unheeded and are casually dismissed as tradition-bound, or arch-conservative.

As fatherhood diminishes, mother-nature becomes more central. Hence the intense, sometimes extreme, interest in ecology, the environment, and planet earth. The disappearance of the vertical dimension has led to an exaltation of the horizontal. The relationship with God the Father has been replaced by relationships between kindred groups bearing various, often elongated acronyms. Godfried Cardinal Danneels' questions are worth pondering: "This feverish search for all sorts of communities, large and small—could it have anything to do with the obliteration of the Father? Is universal brotherhood possible in the absence of a common Father?" (*Handing on the Faith in an Age of Disbelief*). The key word here, is "feverish". For the Belgian Cardinal, it implies a kind of desperation.

The type of community group to which Archbishop Danneels is referring, tends to be self-justifying. Its members are usually protective of each other and abhor any criticism from the outside. They do not have lofty aspirations but merely ask for acceptance. Such an arrangement is the antithesis of Christian community that does not dissolve its relationship with God the Father. The Gospel tells us, "Be perfect, as your heavenly Father is perfect" (Mt 5:48), and "when you have done all that is commanded of you, say, 'We are unworthy servants'" (Lk 17:10).

The Father can command, because He is the loving authority who has given us our life. But He can also forgive us our trespasses and restore us to spiritual health. Without the Father, therefore, three important factors are absent, the gift of life, the command to use it well, and the readiness to forgive. A community lacking in these three factors, even if it calls itself a brotherhood or a coalition or an alliance, is, by comparison, impoverished.

John the Evangelist, in his First Letter (Jn 2:1-2), speaks to us with great solicitude and warmth: "My little children, I am writing to you so that you may not sin; but if any one does sin, we have an advocate with the Father, Jesus the righteous; and he is the expiation for our sins, and not for ours only but also for the sins of the world". All forgiveness is from the Father, whose concern extends to everyone, everywhere.

Brotherhood needs Fatherhood just as children need parents. The rejection of God the Father will continue to have calamitous results. Brotherhood is of the present. Fatherhood not only unites us with the past and with the future, but with eternity.

THE REJECTION OF TRUTH

Central to the story line of Ray Bradbury's celebrated 1953 novel, *Fahrenheit 451*, is a curious reversal that fascinated the author. In the story, firemen, who are traditionally trained to put out fires, start fires. In Bradbury's futuristic world books are illegal, since they cause some people to feel superior to others, and therefore must be destroyed. The idea that books, that should be read, must be destroyed, is another example of this strange reversal of things. In the novel, fireman go from house to house, ferreting out literary contraband and set it on fire. Interestingly enough, the author had experienced a similar reversal when he was accosted by a police officer one night when he was merely walking with a friend and minding his own business. Police, of course, should be helping, not harassing citizens. With mock sincerity, Bradbury promised the policeman never to walk again. But the germ of this odd practice of doing the opposite of what you are supposed to do had been planted in his fertile brain.

What kind of future world did Bradbury envision where firemen start fires and policemen accost innocent citizens? Was this noted author on to something? He has been credited with predicting a number of innovations such as flat screen televisions, automated bank machines, electronic surveillance, thimble radios, and self-driving cars. Did the revered writer of science-fiction (who insisted that he never wrote "science fiction") anticipate that one day reversing one's sworn duties would become pandemic? We may not be able to answer this question satisfactorily. Nonetheless, we witness reversals of responsibilities that now constitute not only a major problem in our brave new world, but also a threat to civilization.

The most glaring reversal took place in 1973 when seven Supreme Court judges found in the United States Constitution a justification for killing unborn human beings. It took special eyesight to find this provision since the very Preamble to the Constitutions states that it exists in order to "establish justice, insure domestic Tranquility, . . . promote the general Welfare, and secure the Blessings of Liberty to ourselves and our Posterity . . ." They found it, nonetheless. It had been hiding for nearly 200 years, "implied in the penumbra," has Harry Blackmun stated. Judges, sworn to uphold the Constitution were actually opposing it. They were now seeing things that were not there, painting by penumbras, as it were.

Robert H. Bork was defeated in his bid to become a Supreme Court justice essentially because he respected the Constitution and called *Roe v. Wade* unconstitutional. His defeat was led by "Roman Catholic" senators Ted Kennedy, Joe Biden, and Pat Leahy. Judges opposing the Constitution were complemented by Catholics opposing life. Reversals were being reinforced by more reversals. As President Reagan, who had nominated Bork, later remarked, "I believe, as he does, [Robert Bork] that judges are to interpret rather than rewrite the Constitution the Founding Fathers crafted with such care and precision."

Judge Bork went on to write *The Tempting of America* (1990) in which he stated rather matter-of-factly, "the right to abort, whatever one thinks of it, is not to be found in the Constitution." In dissent, Justice White had been similarly emphatic: "I find nothing in the language or history of the Constitution to support the Court's judgment." The reversal of integrity is tantamount to tyranny.

We know of priests who promote euthanasia and abortion. Health agencies are now prescribing RU-486, a dangerous drug that has claimed the lives of at least 19 adult lives in recent years. We have school teachers who are required to promote lies and distortions, publishing houses that refuse to publish books that bear witness to Christian values, and politicians who have become enemies of the family. These reversals have caused a widespread distrust of people in authority. What makes the situation even worse is the fact that people with integrity are being persecuted for opposing this wave of tyranny.

Reversing these reversals and restoring integrity among professionals is a daunting task. It will require a new kind of solidarity among grassroots people, family members, plus anyone who is realistic to understand the current threats to the family and civilization. Something of this nature is going on presently in Ontario. Parents opposed to the Liberal government's radical sex education program organized a multi-city Awareness Car Rally that was held in the Greater Toronto Area on August 1, 2015. Cars were decked out with red flags that read: "No to irresponsible sex education," or "My child my choice". The battle lines have been established. The Liberal government has launched a $1.8 million summer ad campaign promoting the sex-ed curriculum. How does one win a war against a government that has unlimited assets at its disposal. "I don't have $1.8 million dollars to work with," voiced a spokesperson for the Parents Alliance of Ontario, "but I do have 1.8 million parents to support us."

We now live under the rule of a professional oligarchy. It is the great task of the people, especially family members, to regain a democratic form of government. The use of the Internet, the distribution of circulars, town meetings, and other ways of informing people that bypass a meretricious Media, will continue to be necessary. It is also urgent that Churches play a more vital role the restoration of democracy of respect for its citizens.

PART TWO
REFLECTIONS ON LIFE

CHAPTER SIX
LIVING AS A PERSON

REALISM

T he advice that we should become who we are is far more profound than most people might realize. For a philosopher, especially one of a Thomist stripe, it is a veritable goldmine, involving explorations into metaphysics, morality, and Christian existentialism.

The first thing that the phrase denotes is that there is a difference between our being and our actions. The two do not necessarily coincide. Moreover, between the two can be either concord or discord. Our being is what grounds us in reality. It has, therefore, metaphysical significance. It differentiates us from all other kinds of beings. It is our natural endowment. Our actions, on the other hand, can be either at variance with our being or consonant with it. When people admonish us for "not being ourselves," they are alluding to the fact that what we are doing is not consistent with who we are in our being. "I wasn't myself," a person might say. Being true to one's self indicates that there is a harmony between a person's *being* and his *actions*."

The rift between a person's *being* and his *actions* is the basis for morality. We have a fundamental duty to be ourselves, which is to say that we should make sure that our actions are congruent with our being. "Human being" is a biological classification; "being human" is a moral imperative. As the great Catholic philosopher, Jacques Maritain, puts it, "man must complete, through his own will, what is sketched in his nature". The *being* we have is not finished. It falls to us to "become who we are" by making proper choices. It is metaphysically futile to try to become a different being, although many people try very hard to achieve this impossibility. The only person we can become is the one whose actions are in accord with our being. In the world of Christian existentialism, the word "authentic" comes into play to describe the person whose moral actions bring to light the depth of his being. The word "integrity" also applies here.

Animals other than man do not possess this rift. And, therefore, they are said to enjoy a certain innocence. A dog cannot help but being a dog. A chameleon may change his colors, but cannot change his nature. Aesop tells the story of the horse that wanted to sing like a nightingale, but this fable merely indicates the hopelessness of trying to become a different being than the one that grounds you in reality. "Become who you are" does not apply to brute animals.

Language attests to the radical moral uniqueness of man. The word "inhuman" means that a person is acting contrary to his being. By contrast, the word "humane" means there is a happy agreement between one's being and his actions. We do not expect lions and kangaroos to be anything than themselves. A lion cannot be "inlion" or "lionane," nor can a kangaroo be "inkangaroonian" or kangarene. Lions and kangaroos are predictably and persistently merely lions and kangaroos.

The notion of *wholeness* captures the kind of person whose actions flow from and are consistent with his being. This word, significantly enough, is etymologically related to "holiness" (as well as "heal," "hale," and "health"). One more thing must be said, however, about "wholeness". As Jacques Maritain, states the matter in somewhat paradoxical terms, "Man is an open whole". What he means by this is that the whole person reaches out to others from the fundamental generosity of his being. He is not closed in on himself. He reaches out through love. In his book, *Existence and the Existent*, we find Maritain expressing the unity of being and becoming in a rather dramatic manner: "Thus it is that when a man has been really awakened to the sense of being or existence, and grasps intuitively the obscure, living depth of the Self and subjectivity, he discovers by the same token the basic generosity of existence and realises, by virtue of this intuition, that love is not a passing pleasure or emotion, but the very meaning of his being alive".

We human being are made to love. Our moral mandate is to actualize the potential that lies in our being, for in our being is our destiny written. We move toward that destiny by choosing, enlightened by reason, what is good. Hence, the importance of prudence, the virtue that allows us to examine all the pertinent facts and circumstances and consistently choose what is good. The *Catholic Catechism* refers to prudence as the "charioteer of the virtues" because it steers other virtues, especially the cardinal virtues of justice, fortitude and temperance, in the right direction. Prudence, then, is the power to make an enlightened choice that is consistent with one's being and related to a moral good.

"Become who you are" is a wake-up call for anyone who wants to enjoy the fullness of life. Most of us slumber and are reluctant to answer the call to fulfill, through our actions, what is dormant in our being. Soren Kierkegaard wrote extensively about the prevalence of despair among those human beings who, consciously or unconsciously, had decided not to be themselves. "The specific character of despair," he wrote, is precisely this: it is unaware of being despair." "Most men lead lives of quiet desperation," added Henry David Thoreau, "and go to the grave with the song still in them". Becoming who we are, maturing as authentic human beings is not any easy task, though it is an essential one. We need the help and inspiration of others, for the quality of our love is an indication of the depth of our being. We all have a song to sing which should not be muted by moral inertia.

Desiderata

Go placidly amid the noise and the haste, & remember
what peace there may be in silence. As far as possible
without surrender be on good terms with all persons.
Speak your truth quietly & clearly; and listen to others,
even the dull and ignorant; they too have their story.
Avoid loud and aggressive persons they are vexatious
to the spirit. If you compare yourself with others
you may become vain and bitter; for always there will be
greater and lesser persons than yourself. Enjoy your
achievements as well as your plans. Keep interested
in your career however humble it is a real possession
in the changing fortunes of time. Exercise caution
in your business affairs for the world is full of
trickery. But let this not blind you to what virtue
there is; many persons strive for high ideals; and
everywhere life is full of heroism. Be yourself. Especially
do not feign affection. Neither be cynical about love;
for in the face of all aridity & disenchantment it is as
perennial as the grass. Take kindly the counsel of the
years. gracefully surrendering the things of youth.
    Nurture strength of spirit to shield you in sudden
    misfortune. But do not distress yourself with
    imaginings. Many fears are born of fatigue and
    loneliness. Beyond a wholesome discipline, be gentle
    with yourself. You are a child of this universe no less
    than the trees and the stars; you have a right to be
    here. And whether or not it is clear to you, no doubt
    the universe is unfolding as it should. Therefore be
    at peace with God, whatever you conceive Him to be.
    And whatever your labors and aspirations, in the noisy
    confusion of life keep peace with your soul.
    With all its sham, drudgery and broken dreams,
        it is still a beautiful world.
            Be cheerful.
        Strive to be happy +

RIGHTS

Whenever we make a big decision, it is wise to do so from a broad perspective. Before proposing marriage or taking a new job, before deciding on the purchase of a house or a car, one should seek the opinions of others and make sure to take sufficient time. A broader perspective than self-interest and the fleeting moment can safeguard us from making bad choices. What we choose out of self-interest is often contrary to what is good for us. What we sew in haste we often reap in regret.

The Desiderata (things we desire), the creation of Max Ehrmann, who labored in relative obscurity during his lifetime, offers us a broad perspective in which we can more accurately weigh the important things in life. Written in 1927, it represents that rare and felicitous combination of inspirational poetry, illuminating philosophy, and widespread popularity.

Presidential hopeful, Adlai Stevenson helped to bring *The Desiderata* to the attention of the public in 1965 when it was learned that he had planned to use it in his Christmas cards. It became an immensely popular poster and was celebrated in songs, magazines, and in motion pictures. Joan Crawford recited it on television. Leonard Nimoy, of Star Trek fame, recorded it on his 1968 album, *Two Sides of Leonard Nimoy*, and again on the 1995 re-release of *Leonard Nimoy Presents Mr. Spock's Music From Outer Space*. Morgan Freeman, in a 2012 interview on Oprah Winfrey's *Master Class Television Special*, expressed how deeply *The Desiderata* shaped his life.

What are the "things we desire? First of all, as the first line of the poem indicates, it is *peace*: "Go placidly amid the noise and haste". But how do we attain peace? Essentially, the poem advises us to look at our life in the context of the unfolding universe. Here, the author is borrowing from the 17th century philosopher, Benedict Spinoza, who taught that we could calm our spirit if we looked at things from the perspective of eternity (*sub specie aeternitatis*). In other words, by taking the long view of things, locating ourselves in the vast scheme of events, our momentary problems seem to be utterly unimportant. This philosophy seemed to benefit Spinoza. Even his enemies regarded him as a "saintly man".

This larger perspective also helps us to find *love*, which, despite one's experience of "aridity and disenchantment" is "as perennial as grass". By maintaining "peace with God" and with our soul, we place ourselves on the road to happiness. As we locate ourselves in the context of an unfolding universe, we begin to see ourselves as its children, and our troubles begin to fade away. Perhaps the most characteristic stanza of *The Desiderata* is the third to the last:

> You are a child of the universe.
> No less than the trees and the stars
> You have a right to be here.
> And whether or not it is clear to you,
> No doubt the universe is unfolding
> As it should.

It is most interesting to note that many who treasured *The Desiderata* missed its implications for the right of the unborn child to "be here". When Canada's government lost its majority in the federal election of 1972, Prime Minister Pierre Trudeau reassured the nation that "The universe is unfolding as it should". It is supremely ironic that it was Trudeau who introduced abortion legislation, asserting that thousands of unborn babies *do not* have a right to be here."

Surely, if "the trees and the stars" have a right to be here, that same right should be extended to unborn human beings. For Ehrmann, not only are we children of parents, but, in the context of an unfolding universe, we are the offspring of all our previous parents in that long line that goes back to our primordial ancestors. When we think that the merging of just one of millions or spermatozoa with just one of thousands of eggs were needed to produce our unique selfhood, it seems improbable that we should be here exactly as we are. Then, when we multiply this improbability by all our preceding ancestors, it becomes, when we try to think of it, a mental preoccupation that, in the words of John Keats, "dost tease us out of thought as doth eternity". We find ourselves outside the limits of comprehension, though at the same time, filled with awe at a phenomenon that transcends our capacity for understanding. The universe has been the patient parent that has led, over millennia, through one stupendous improbability after another, to the appearance of a particular unborn child. Yet, in the narrow perspective of convenience and the pressure of the moment, it is denied its right to be here and is rejected.

Abortion, it would seem, means that the universe is not unfolding as it should. What is the moral significance of being a part of this evolving universe? For Ehrmann, it is appreciation and acceptance of what time and nature have brought into being. "Take kindly the counsel of the years" suggests that we learn from the past, from history, from the way eternity expresses itself from one epoch to another.

We are, indeed, children of the universe. In this larger perspective, we learn something about the Wisdom of God and the foolishness of man. *The Desiderata* should be granted a revival for a world that is immersed in the moment and lost for lack of vision.

HUMANITARIANISM

The story is told of a great feast that was to be held in a medieval village. To insure its success, a huge cask was built into which each participant was to pour a bottle of wine. One villager, thinking to himself that one bottle of water would go unnoticed in a sea of wine, poured in his share of the more common and less expensive beverage. When the big day arrived, the cask was tapped. But all that flowed from it was water, Adam's ale, *aqua pura*, H20. Each participant reasoned the same way, "My small contribution would be drowned out by the contributions of others."

This story illustrates the selfishness not only of the individual but of a whole community of individuals. It is the kind of story that feeds the notion that, after all, people are only human, and they tend to think of themselves first at the expense of others. It gives permission to use one's humanity as an excuse for one's wrongdoing.

But it is not humanity that is at fault. Human nature should not take the blame. One may say, "What do you expect, I am only human." Yet, one never hears a person say, "I am not a humanitarian because, after all, I am only human." Here, the contradiction between one's nature and errant behavior becomes more apparent. The pagan philosopher Terence put things in the proper perspective when he said, "I am a human being: I regard nothing of human interest as foreign to me" (*"Homo sum: humani nil a me alienum puto."*). This Latin thinker understood the profound and obligatory bond between being a human being and involving oneself in human concerns. He would, most likely have added his best bottle of wine to the great cask at the medieval feast.

Perhaps no one expressed the matter more eloquently than Hamlet, who, despite his sour mood, spoke of man in glorious terms: "What a piece of work is a man! How noble in reason, how infinite in faculty! In form and moving how express and admirable! In action how like an Angel! in apprehension how like a god! The beauty of the world! The paragon of animals! . . . [the] quintessence of dust?"

The last phrase warrants amplification. The ancient Greeks believed the world to be composed of four elements: air, earth, fire, and water. The fifth essence (*quinta essentia*) was imperishable and believed to be the substance of the imperishable stars. Man is a paradox, therefore, a composite of a perishable body and an imperishable soul. Therefore, man can be viewed in two radically different ways: as being mistake prone or as aspiring to the heavens. Gerard Manley Hopkins took the high road, referring to man as "immortal diamond".

The distinguished French existentialist philosopher, Gabriel Marcel, writes of a remarkable experience he had. "I was coming home from a concert," he wrote, "where I had heard Bach played and I experienced in myself a revival of a feeling or rather of a certainty that seems to have been lost in our time: the honor of being human."

Human beings are dispatched these days, through abortion and euthanasia, with increasing ease. Was Marcel right? Have we, indeed, we citizens of the modern world, lost that sense of "the honor of being human"? The temptation to suicide among high school students, according to recent sociological studies is alarmingly high. Do these students understand the great honor it is to be a human being? Or are they more interested in getting ahead, looking better than others, or being popular? The best of art reminds us of our unalienable dignity as human beings. It reminds us of what our focus should be.

I have been informed that in some zoos throughout the world, humans are now on display along with other species of the animal kingdom. The honor of being human, of course, is not something that can be observed by onlookers. It is something that one can sense, and with certainty, within himself. Bing Crosby, in the 1944 movie, *Going My Way*, used his enchanting voice to convey a message to each boy in his charge that "you can be better off than you are" because you can do great things that animals cannot possibly do. You can "swing on a star, carry moon beams home in a jar". You do not want to be a "mule" or a "pig" or a "fish" or a "monkey". If you "hate to go to school you may grow up to be a mule"; "if you don't care a feather or a fig, you may grow up to be a pig"; "if that sort of life is what you wish, you may grow up to be a fish." Nor is the monkey worthy of emulation. In closing his musical instruction, without ignoring the human paradox, the inimitable crooner tells the youth of America:

"So, you see it's all up to you. You can be better than you are. You could be swinging on a star."

We should not blame human nature for our failings, for it is up to us to follow our better angels, the loftier impulses of our humanity. We need not follow the example of the medieval villagers, but listen to the philosophy of Terence and Marcel, the poetry of Shakespeare and Hopkins, the music of Bach and, yes, even that of a blue-eyed baritone more formally known as Harry Lillis Crosby, Jr.

THE GIFT OF KNOWLEDGE

CONSCIENCE

My earliest recollection of an explanation of conscience was when I was a young lad sitting in a movie theater and being enthralled by Walt Disney's 1940 classic, *Pinocchio*. The newly carved puppet had been brought to life by the Blue Fairy. But he was still a puppet and had not been endowed with a conscience. It fell to Jiminy Cricket to instruct Pinocchio on the meaning of conscience.

"If you want to be a real boy," Jiminy explained, "you have to know how to do the right thing because the world is full of temptations". Therefore, you must "always let your conscience be your guide". Then, the conscientious cricket launched into his explanation of conscience: "the wrong things that seem right at the time but even though the right things may seem wrong sometimes, sometimes the wrong things maybe right at the wrong time or *vice versa*. Understand?" Master Cricket may have been less a disciple of St. Thomas Aquinas than a forerunner of the late great, Yogi Berra, who once explained to his troops that "good pitching beats good hitting every time, and *vice versa*."

Pinocchio, needless to say, is dumbfounded. Yet, despite the cricket's convoluted gobbledygook, this amusing cinematic segment made two things clear to me: 1) that you must have a properly functioning conscience in order to be a complete person; 2) that although conscience is essential for a good life, it is very difficult to explain. And now that I have arrived at man's estate, I endeavor to offer a clearer explanation of conscience than what the dutiful Professor Cricket had to offer. But what can we expect from a cricket?

The first thing to know about conscience is contained in the very etymology of the word. "Conscience" means *con + scientia*, or "with knowledge". Consequently, knowledge serves as the basis for conscience.

There can be no correct formation of conscience without knowledge. This knowledge is objective and reliable. In a word, it represents truth. The great paradox of conscience is that although it abides within us, even at the core of our personality, it is tied to the external world of truth. Conscience is neither purely subjective not purely objective; it is like the living current that flows from the opposite poles of a battery. Conscience connects us with the world of moral values.

This *truth* is not invented, but discovered. Conscience does not make laws; it respects them. Saint John Paul's phrase, *Veritatis Splendor* (the title of his most morality centered encyclical), indicates that truth has a certain splendor or light by which it can be recognized. Truth should not be regarded as obscure, hidden, or confusing. Truth greets the mind as light enters the eye. Conscience, then, does not create norms, but discovers them in the objective order of morality.

Conscience needs truth in order to function. But it has an equal reliance on freedom. Let us imagine a triangle whose three sides are composed of truth, freedom, and conscience. Without truth, we have impulse, urge, feeling, hunch, caprice, guess, or whim. Nietzsche exemplified this error when he substituted "sublimated instinct" for conscience.

On the other hand, without freedom we have a requirement, an imperative, necessity, imposition, demand, compulsion, or determination. Here, Sigmund Freud constructed the "super-ego" as an unavoidable compromise between the demands of instinct and the restrictions of society. For the pioneer of modern psychology, there was no room for freedom.

If we reduce the triangle to three separate and independent lines, we find that truth, freedom, and conscience go nowhere. People love freedom, but they often do not understand it. They love conscience, but often separate it from its rectifying basis. They love truth, but only when it serves their individual purposes.

Conscience without truth is blind; conscience without freedom is compulsion. Conscience, then, is the faculty or power within us that is capable of a free and creative acceptance of the truth which serves as a guide for our moral actions. Let us offer but one example. We know that the truth about marriage excludes adultery, since adultery can be destructive of the faithful bond that exists between husband and wife.

When conscience freely accepts this truth, it informs us to accept the truth about marriage and avoid or reject adultery. When we act contrary to what we know to be right, we experience guilt. Guilt, then, is nothing more than the recognition of our complicity in wrongdoing. It is the recognition that our faults are not in the stars, but in us.

Saint John Paul II has identified conscience in a most helpful as well as eloquent way. Conscience, he writes, is "the sacred core and sanctuary of man, where he is alone with God, whose voice echoes in his depth". We should not be listening to the voice of the masses or the siren song of secular society, or the arbitrary constructions of political correctness. God is the author of the moral order and in attending to it, we are at the same time, listening to Him.

We must be conscientious about conscience for it is our guide, our glory, and our gift from God.

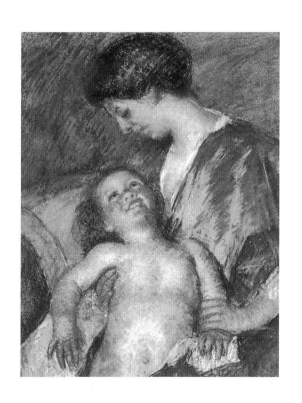

ACCEPTANCE

Perhaps more has been written about motherhood than on any other subject. Given the dignity and importance of motherhood, this is both understandable and justifiable. Nonetheless, more will continue to be written about motherhood because its depth can never be exhausted.

The eminent theologian Hans Urs von Balthasar opens the third volume of his *Explorations in Theology* with this intriguing sentence: "The little child awakens to self-consciousness through being addressed by the love of his mother." From a biological point of view, the child's parents account for his existence. But the child's awareness that he is a unique self, von Balthasar explains, is the work of the mother.

How does she do this? If we may borrow the "I-Thou" terminology of Martin Buber, the mother is the "Thou" who, through her tender love, awakens the "I" of the child to self-consciousness. The child becomes aware that he is a partner in a love-to-love relationship. The mother's love elicits a response which is the child's love. The child's response is spontaneous. He does not consider whether to respond to his mother's love with love or something else. His response is antecedent to any reflection. His core nature as a being of love, one created by a loving God, is touched. His response is a pure indication of his nature. He responds with love because his mother's gift of love is not something that he can refuse. Just as the sun entices green growth, the mother's love summons forth the child's love, thus completing the "I-Thou" bond.

But there is something far more profound that occurs in the mother-child relationship. As von Balthasar states, the mother's love is delivered as a "lightning flash of the origin with a ray so brilliant and whole that it also includes a disclosure of God". This helps to explain what Saint John Paul meant when he remarked that "an ounce of mother is worth a ton of priests". God has an "I-Thou" relationship with man. However, the adult response to God's love usually requires reflection and decision-making.

But the early loving response of the child to his mother's love is something that the adult can build on. Along with mother's milk, the mother is awakening in her child, a sense of God.

The child interprets his mother's smiling and her whole gift of self as coming from another, thereby distinguishing the "Thou" of the mother from the "I" of the child. In this way, the love-to-love bond is achieved. The child responds to his mother's love with love of his own, thus awakening him to the realization, however dim, that he is made to love. This is a moment that is central and sacred to human beings. It is their origin and starting point. It is more fundamentally humanizing than any other human relationship.

A British poet by the name of Anne Ridler (1912-2001), who at one time served as a secretary for T. S. Eliot, authored 11 volumes of poetry over a 50-year span. A mother to two sons and as many daughters, she has penned a number of poems that reveal her own acute sensitivity to the mother-child relationship. In *Choosing a Name*, she beautifully expresses the mother-child relationship to which von Balthasar alludes, where generous love embraces receptive child:

Frail vessel, launched with a shawl for sail,
Whose guiding spirit keeps his needle-quivering
Poise between trust and terror,
And stares amazed to find himself alive;
This is the means by which you say *I am*.

As Mrs. Ridler implies, love summons "trust," whereas its absence suggests "terror". Motherhood is the gift of self that summons a loving response that requires no deliberation but comes straight from the heart. It is an example and prototype that we can never exhaust, but must continually honor.

CHAPTER SEVEN
LIVING A LIFE OF MERCY

MERCY'S DISTINCTIVENESS

In the world of amateur baseball there is something called "the mercy rule". It is applied when a losing team is trailing by as many as fifteen runs. The purpose of the rule is to end the suffering and humiliation of the players on a team that no longer has any hope of winning. The rule is unobjectionable when it is applied to baseball. In fact, it might even be regarded as admirable and humane. But it is quite another thing when it is applied to life. For many people, especially those who promote euthanasia, mercy means ending the suffering and humiliation of a person by ending his life. The well-known phrase, "mercy killing," is a rationalization that attempts to make killing another person appear to be a virtuous act.

Mercy, properly speaking, is a virtue. It is a tribute to virtue when one uses the name of a virtue to justify an evil act. "Mercy killing" has the pretense of a virtue without possessing its essence. At the close of his encyclical *The Gospel of Life (Evangelium Vitae)*, Saint John Paul II invokes Mary to intercede for "the elderly and the sick killed by indifference or out of misguided mercy." For every genuine virtue there is a counterfeit counterpart. This is particularly evident with respect to compassion which is commonly employed as a justification for abortion.

True mercy is always on the side of life. St. Thomas Aquinas defines mercy as "the compassion in our hearts (*"misericordia"*) for another person's misery." Had he concluded his definition at that point, he would have been sorely remiss and would have given encouragement to advocates of mercy killing. But the second part of his definition is crucial. The Angelic Doctor, citing St. Augustine, states that mercy is "a compassion which drives us to do what we can to help him" (*Summa Theologica* II-II, 30, 1). Mercy, therefore, is both "affective," involving the emotions, as well as "effective," involving practical assistance. Putting a person to death is not a way of helping him.

Mercy may be shown to those who suffer through no fault of their own. Nonetheless, in the Year of Mercy, a special emphasis is given to those who suffer as a consequence of sin. Pope Francis stressed this aspect of mercy when he accepted the papacy: "This is me, a sinner on whom the Lord has turned his gaze. And this is what I said when they asked me if I would accept my election as pontiff. I am a sinner, but I trust in the infinite mercy and patience of our Lord Jesus Christ." Pope Francis' declaration is remarkably similar to that of another visionary, Christopher Columbus: "I am a most noteworthy sinner, but I have cried out to the Lord for grace and mercy, and they have covered me completely. I have found the sweetest consolation since I made my whole purpose to enjoy His marvelous Presence." Novelist Herman Melville made the same point though far more dramatically. "Heaven have mercy on us all," he wrote, for we are all somehow dreadfully cracked about the head, and sadly need mending." Another celebrated novelist, Charles Dickens, confessed that, "but for the mercy of God, I might easily have been, for any care that was taken of me, a little robber or a vagabond." "The wonderful news," declares evangelist Billy Graham, "is that our Lord is a God of mercy, and He responds to repentance."

Mercy should not be misguided. It should be beneficial. But it should not be doled out irresponsibly. Mercy is a mutual affair. The recipient must have the right disposition in order to receive and benefit from mercy. The celebrated mystery writer Agatha Christie understood well that when mercy is dispensed recklessly, irrespective of justice, it can prove to be counterproductive. "Too much mercy," she remarked, "often resulted in further crimes which were fatal to innocent victims who need not have been victims if justice had been put first and mercy second." It belongs to wisdom to place things in their proper order.

The sinner is not eligible for mercy unless he is willing to accept justice. Mercy, therefore, does not stand alone. Justice alone can be cold legalism, whereas mercy alone can be meaningless. In Shakespeare's famous panegyric to mercy that appears in *The Merchant of Venice*, he points out that mercy is "the throned monarch better than his crown." The "crown" is a symbol of justice and temporal power. But mercy is personal and "is enthroned in the hearts of kings". When he states that "mercy seasons justice" he is affirming the validity of both virtues, while putting them in their proper order.

The anatomy of mercy reveals an interesting variety of twists and turns, curves and contours. It should be, at the same time, both passionate and practical. It should be in the interest of life, not death. It can restore sinners to a life of grace. It is available to all who suffer, whether their suffering is deserved or undeserved. It is higher than justice, but nonetheless presupposes it. It is dispensed with a generous heart. It blesses both the giver as well as the receiver. It is virtuous only when it is whole, when all its composing parts are properly integrated. It can easily become a vice when it is fragmented for convenience. A Year of Mercy, let us hope, will result in a Life of Grace.

MERCY'S IMPORTANCE

There can be no question that mercy is a beautiful virtue and that it is an attribute of God. It is also a virtue that is urgently needed in our sinful and broken world. At the same time, it is important to note that it is not the only virtue and not the only attribute of God. Dionysius, in his classic work *On the Divine Names* includes Holiness, Beauty, Goodness, Light, Omnipotence, and other names to represent God. God is also love, justice, wisdom, and truth. For St. Francis even courtesy is an attribute of God (*La cortesia e una proprieta di Dio*).

Pope Francis' new book, *A Year of Mercy with Pope Francis: Daily Reflections*, is not a systematic treatise on mercy. It is, as one reviewer states, a series of "bite-sized quotes and engaging questions [that] will fit easily into your busy schedule." The book is a best-seller. Furthermore, it has been a source of inspiration and comfort to an untold number of readers, Catholic as well as non-Catholic. Yet, it has caused some readers to wonder if the message implies that we can do whatever we want and still be eligible for mercy.

The Catholic who wants to understand the notion of mercy more fully will benefit greatly by reading Saint John Paul II's encyclical *Dives Misericordia* (*Rich in Mercy*). It should be remembered that the former pontiff was devoted to promoting mercy. He designated the second Sunday of Easter to be Divine Mercy Sunday, making this announcement at the canonization of Sister Faustina Kowalska who inaugurated the spiritual movement of Divine Mercy. On that occasion John Paul stated that this Feast Day represents "a perpetual invitation to the Christian world to address, with trust in divine benevolence, the difficulties and trials that await the human race in the coming years." This statement could just as easily have been written by the present pope. It is worth mentioning that Saint John Paul passed away at 2:37 EST on April 2, 2005, the Vigil of Divine Mercy Sunday.

In *Dives in Misericordia*, Saint John Paul is at pains to clarify the notion of mercy. He points out that in revealing his love/mercy, "God, at the same time demanded from people that they also should be guided in their lives by love and mercy." God is merciful, but He is also "demanding". In His Sermon on the Mount, Christ proclaimed: "Blessed are the merciful, for they shall obtain mercy." In this way, the Messianic message preserves a Divine-human relationship. In other words, the merciful shall receive mercy. Hence the obligation on the part of human beings to be merciful to others as a condition for receiving mercy themselves. God is rich in mercy, but it is dispensed to those who themselves are merciful. God's mercy, therefore, does not stand alone, its blessing depends on the merciful hearts of its benefactors.

Our reception of God's mercy presupposes our own expression of mercy. In addition, there is something that should follow this reception, namely reform. The people of the Old Covenant experienced misery from the time they worshiped the Golden calf. This did not please the Lord, who said to Moses that He is a "God merciful and gracious, slow to anger, and abounding in steadfast love and faithfulness." As Saint John Paul writes, "Even when the Lord is exasperated by the infidelity of His people and thinks of finishing with it, it is still His tenderness and generous love for those who are His own which overcomes His anger." Whereas people may abandon God, God will never abandon His people. Mercy, then, has a twofold purpose: 1) It is an instrument of forgiveness; 2) It provides grace for reform. Mercy remains unfulfilled where its recipient does not reform his life.

If mercy stood alone, isolated from human mercy and human reform, it would be as worthless as counterfeit money. Bogus currency is not backed by the government. Hence, it cannot be validly issued. Secondly, it has no purchasing power and therefore, it does not enrich its possessor.

Saint John Paul II also writes about the importance of justice. There can be no justice without mercy. In the words of St. Thomas Aquinas, "mercy without justice is the mother of dissolution. Justice without mercy is cruelty." The parable of the Prodigal Son is one of the most moving stories in the New Testament. Nonetheless, the son became eligible for his father's mercy only once he was repentant and acknowledged his sinfulness. He was finally able to recognize that his sins against God were injustices against Him. It is a beautiful story because it harmonizes repentance, justice, forgiveness, mercy, and reform. God is merciful, but we must ask for it by being merciful and just ourselves, and willing to amend our lives.

Pope Francis' style and approach, we might say, is more immediate, pastoral, and easy to grasp. The style and approach of Saint John Paul II, by contrast, is more systematic, philosophical, and more difficult to grasp. Together, however, somewhat like Plato and Aristotle, they complement each other and provide a more complete picture. We should not ignore the great contribution that Pope Francis' predecessor has made in promoting the virtue of mercy. Church teaching enjoys the blessing of continuity. It is in that larger scope that we find answers that we might not be able to locate within one time period or from a single author. As Saint John Paul has selflessly proclaimed, "The Church must profess and proclaim God's mercy in all its truth, as it has been handed down to us by revelation."

MERCY'S RICHNESS

Today is November 30, a fitting day to write about mercy. It was on this final day of the 11th month of the year in 1980 that Saint John Paul II published his second encyclical, *Dives in Misericordia* ("Rich in Mercy"). It serves as excellent prelude to and preparation for a better understanding of the year-long celebration of the Jubilee of Mercy proclaimed by Pope Francis for 2016. In the words of the reigning pontiff, "The Church must be a place of mercy freely given, where everyone can feel welcomed, loved, forgiven, and encouraged to live the good life of the Gospel".

Thirty-five years is roughly the equivalent of a generation. The Church's affirmation of the importance of mercy is hardly new, though its emphasis over the years can easily be forgotten or ignored. In the fourth century, for example, St. Ambrose stated something that would have caused Saint John Paul to rejoice: "Mercy, also, is a good thing, for it makes men perfect, in that it imitates the perfect Father. Nothing graces the Christian soul so much as mercy." The world is in the business of "news," delivering "today's news today". The Church has a much broader view of things. We should recall what Christ told us more than 2,000 years ago: "Blessed are the merciful, for they shall obtain mercy" (I Corinthians, 4, 1).

Saint John Paul begins the most intensely theological of his encyclicals by announcing to the world that "God is rich in mercy" and the one to whom "Jesus Christ has revealed to us as Father: It is His very Son who, in Himself, has manifested Him and made Him known to us." God is the "Father of mercies," a truth that should be a source of hope and consolation for all who are suffering. "In the context of today's threats to man," the mercy of God makes "a unique appeal addressed to the Church."

Krakow, Poland was the center of the "Divine Mercy" devotion promoted by Faustina Kowalska. Sister Faustina had a series of mystical experiences through which she believed that she was called to renew the Church's devotion to God's mercy. The "Merciful Jesus" icon associated with her message shows Christ in a white garment with two rays emanating from his breast. It represents a vision she had on February 22, 1931. Saint John Paul acknowledged that he felt "very near" to Sister Faustina and had been "thinking about her for a long time" prior to writing *Dives in Misericordia*.

Another important influence in writing his encyclical is the notion of fatherhood, one that had captured his imagination and ripened over the years. Life with his own father and Cardinal Sapieha had given him a strong sense of both familial and spiritual paternity. He also thought of his own priesthood as a form of paternity.

Central the Saint John Paul's encyclical is the parable of the prodigal son, an account that reveals the mercy of the father, a virtue that belongs to the essence of fatherhood. The father fully recognizes the waywardness of his son. More importantly, however, he recognizes the fundamental good and dignity of his humanity. The son invites mercy because he has returned home and has repudiated his sinful ways. The father awaits the return of his son with hope, rushes toward his long lost son when he does return, and embraces him with love. The son has squandered his inheritance. But his humanity is saved.

"Love is 'greater' than justice," writes the late pontiff, because it is primary and fundamental". Yet justice plays a crucial role in relation to the dispensation and acceptance of mercy. "Mercy is the fulfillment of justice, not its abolition," St. Thomas Aquinas states in his *Summa Theologica* (I, 21, 3). Mercy cannot be given, willy-nilly to the unrepentant. They do not want mercy because they have rejected justice. Love is more fundamental than mercy, but so is justice. The prodigal son saw the truth of his errant ways. He did not rationalize or deny them. His acceptance of justice rendered him eligible for the acceptance of mercy.

This point is well dramatized in Heinrich von Kleist's play, *Prince Frederick of Homburg*. Frederick William, the Elector of Brandenburg's son, Prince Frederick of Homburg, disobeys an important military order. He is subsequently tried and condemned to die. For some time, the son refuses to acknowledge that his sentence was just. Finally, he comes to the realization that his disobedience and concern for self-glory fully warranted the death penalty. At that point, his joyful father tears up the death sentence and pardons his son. The Prince was eligible for his father's mercy only when he was willing to accept justice. As Shakespeare adds, "Mercy seasons justice."

The prodigal son and the Prince in Kleist's play represent a kind of Everyman who, owing to human weakness, strays from righteousness. The faithful fathers in both of these stories, go beyond justice, without abandoning it, and restore their sons to the fundamental truths of their humanity. True mercy in no way humiliates or makes passive its recipient. Rather it confirms him in his dignity and humanity. Through mercy, inspired by love, human dignity is regained. Saint Bernard, in his Sermons on the *Canticle of Canticles* put the matter quite poetically when he wrote: "Happy is the soul who has made it her business to collect miseries, to pour on them the oil of mercy and heat them on the fire of love!"

If we want mercy, we should be merciful to our neighbor. The Year of Mercy should be the year when we behave more mercifully to others.

"The most merciful thing that the large family does to one of its members is to kill it."

Margaret Sanger
Founder
Planned Parenthood

"We are truly grateful to you. Thank you, Planned Parenthood. God bless you."

Barack Obama
President
United States

MERCY'S AVAILABILITY

"**Why is there a Church?**" Cardinal Pell has answered this often asked question in a timely and theologically sound way. The Church exists, says the Australian prelate, to bring God's mercy into the world. Two essential points are implied by this comment. The first is that mercy is available. God is Mercy and His Mercy has no limit. It is infinite. The second is that if mercy is to be dispensed, it must first be requested. If mercy is not requested, it is not received.

The distinction between the availability and reception of mercy calls to mind a remark that the noted evangelist Fr. Vincent McNabb, O.P. made while speaking to a public gathering in London's Speaker's Corner. A heckler interrupted the famous preacher by loudly objecting that if God really existed He would be everywhere and evident to everyone. The perspicacious Dominican noted the protester's face that urgently needed to be washed. Without missing a beat, the unflappable apologist replied that no one would believe that a man's dirty face implied that water did not exist.

A pizza emporium has pizza readily available. But if no one requests it, North America's favorite snack is not delivered. The great problem afflicting mankind is the illusion of self-sufficiency, the notion that we can save ourselves through ourselves and need neither God nor His Mercy. With regard to pizza, good marketing closes the gap between availability and delivery; with regard to human beings, it is humility that closes the gap between God's Mercy and its human reception.

When President Obama exclaims, "God bless Planned Parenthood," he is not invoking God's blessing, but, in effect, asking God to congratulate this abortion conglomeration for the splendid work it is doing. Planned Parenthood could use God's Mercy, but its commitment to violating His Fifth Commandment is incompatible with requesting it. It is a model example for all who use the deception of self-sufficiency as a barrier to God's Grace.

King Frederick William I (1688-1740) once visited a prison in Potsdam, Germany with the hope of dispensing mercy. He listened attentively to one prisoner after another, each of whom claimed that he was a victim of injustice. They all alleged being sent to prison because of prejudiced judges, perjured witnesses, or unscrupulous lawyers. From cell to cell, the King heard each prisoner swear his innocence and insist on his false imprisonment until he came to an inmate who said nothing. "Well, I suppose you are innocent, too," said Frederick, somewhat sarcastically. "No, Your Majesty," came the startling reply. "I am guilty and richly deserve all that I get." "Here, turnkey," thundered the King, "come and get rid of this rascal quick, before he corrupts this fine lot of innocent people that you are responsible for." The King could dispense mercy because this contrite prisoner was disposed to receive it. Availability was not the issue.

How do we, as ordinary Christians dispense mercy, or at least, help others to do so. If I may stretch an analogy, I once found myself in a comparable, but far less dramatic situation than that of King Frederick. While a house guest, I observed an unhappy situation unfolding for which there seemed to be no solution. The oldest daughter had apparently (but not definitively) neglected certain household duties. Her punishment was severe. Should would not be allowed to play soccer that day. The father of the house wanted to be merciful, but he knew that he must also insist on discipline and responsibility. He feared that if he backed down, he would be shirking his fatherly responsibilities. The mother also hoped for mercy, but remained silent since she did not want to interfere with the execution of her husband's responsibilities. It was a stand-off. Meanwhile, I could hear the daughter's sobs surfacing from her prison in the basement.

I thought of a way that would be acceptable to everyone. "There is an old Catholic tradition," I said to my hosts, who were highly respectful of Catholic lore, "that if you are showing hospitality to a guest and it is his birthday (which it was), "in accordance with the esteemed Passover custom, you are allowed to release one prisoner." That did the trick. A broad smile swept across the father's face. He raced downstairs and freed his prisoner. She emerged happily from her cell, gave me a big hug and verbalized her heartfelt thanks. The father could show mercy because he had a basis that justified it, and one that had a long and honored tradition (especially the part about the Passover). We can all help to combine the availability of mercy in one with its reception in another.

Mercy cannot be dispensed willy-nilly. It means nothing to the unrepentant who would regard it as irrelevant and unneeded. But it means everything to the person who has accepted justice and thirsts for mercy. "Justice without mercy is cruelty," writes St. Thomas Aquinas. On the other hand, according to the Angelic Doctor, "Mercy without justice is the mother of dissolution." The New England poet, Henry Wadsworth Longfellow put it nicely when he said, "Being all fashioned of the self-same dust, / Let us be merciful as well as just."

A little mercy goes a long way. It can bring joy to a young girl, relief to a father, pride to a mother, and peace to a family. But it can also bring a smile of satisfaction to a house guest.

MERCY'S WARMTH

When we do not hear another person's words correctly we say, "I beg your pardon". A moderator appears on stage and apologizes for a momentary inconvenience by saying to the audience, "I beg your indulgence". These words flow easily from our lips, usually without much reflection. They have become automatic responses, polite gestures, clichés. On reflection, however, they identify the speakers as "beggars".

Now, we think of beggars as unfortunates with whom we do not identify. And yet, in the eyes of God, we are all beggars, beggars for mercy. We are prone to dividing people by class, wealth, ability, station, and pedigree. Yet, despite our proclivity for feeling superior to others, the one common denominator that unites all of us is that we are all beggars. When we sin, we should say to God, "I beg Your pardon". When we fall, we should say to Him, "I beg your indulgence". Alfred Lord Tennyson, in his poem, "Lady Clara Vere de Vere," shows his contempt for dividing people according to rank when he writes:

> Howe'er it be, it seems to me,
> 'Tis only noble to be good.
> Kind hearts are more than coronets,
> And simple faith than Norman blood.

We often mistake humility for humiliation. Therefore, we might find it humiliating to be characterized as a beggar. But it is an act of humility to see ourselves as beggars before the footstool of Christ. Humility is the virtue that allows us to see ourselves in our truth. Pride is the vice by which we see ourselves as something that we are not. When we receive mercy, our humility is rewarded. Pride is usually followed by a fall.

When Queen Elizabeth donned her coronet, she did so with gratitude for God's Mercy and with service toward others foremost in mind: "Therefore I am sure that this, my Coronation, is not the symbol of a power and a splendor that are gone but a declaration of our hopes for the future, and for the years I may, by God's Grace and Mercy, be given to reign and serve you as your Queen."

Bishop Bruskewitz of Lincoln, Nebraska, illustrates the point that we are all beggars in relating a most interesting account of a meeting between a fallen priest, who had lost his faith and had descended to the level of being a street beggar, and Saint John Paul II. The meeting was set up by a chance encounter between a priest (let us call him Fr. M), who was a friend of the Bishop, and the fallen priest, a former colleague of Fr. M's from the seminary. Being moved by the priest/beggar's plight, Fr. M promised to pray for him. "Lot of good that will do," the beggar cynically replied.

Fr. M, who had been scheduled to meet with the Pope, informed the Holy Father of the encounter he had with his former seminary classmate earlier in the day. The following day, John Paul arranged a dinner for the two priests. Before the meal was over, the Pope asked Fr. M to leave the room. And then, an extraordinary thing happened. The Holy Father asked the beggar to hear his confession! Astonished, the beggar replied, "Me! How could I? I'm just a beggar." The saintly pontiff clasped the man's hands in his and said, "So am I". After hearing the beggar's confession, the Holy Father reinstated the beggar's status as a priest and commissioned him to minister to the other beggars in the parish. "A little bit of mercy makes the world less cold and more just," as Pope Francis would later state.

The virtue of graciousness is closely aligned with that of mercy. It is the perfect opposite of snobbery. The gracious person does not allow social barriers of any form to prevent him from expressing his merciful care for others. The distinguished psychiatrist, Viktor Frankl, personifies this beautiful virtue. One night at about 3:00 AM, he was awakened by a distraught woman who spoke incoherently to him for about twenty minutes. Sometime later, the woman met Frankl and thanked him for saving her life. The eminent doctor confessed that he was too sleepy during her telephone call to have been in any way helpful. "But," she said, "the very fact that a great man such as you would spend twenty minutes on the phone at three o'clock in the morning with a complete stranger such as myself meant that I must be important in some way, and so I decided to go on living." Graciousness is being merciful to strangers as well as to the sick, the needy, and the homeless. God is merciful to us despite the fact that He is the Creator, and we, having been drawn out of nothingness, are is finite creatures.

The best way to be eligible for God's mercy is to be humble, and by that virtue, be united to all others. The best way to be ineligible for God's mercy is to be proud, and by that vice to think of oneself as better than others. The Pope is "the servant of servants". He is the humble servant who serves anyone, and without distinction. It is the view of the world that divides people into those who are superior and those who are inferior. But the world does not seek mercy; it seeks applause. We should praise God and not look to Him to praise us.

CHAPTER EIGHT
LIVING A LIFE OF VIRTUE

THE IMPORTANCE OF PRAYER

In the 2012 movie, *And Now a Word from Our Sponsor*, the CEO of a major advertising agency wakes up in a hospital, but can speak only in advertising slogans. It has been said that this "Word", in a title that has become a household cliché," is the longest "word" in the language. It may be that, but it also may be the barest. Advertising slogans are not intended to elicit a response. In fact, they usually fail to elicit even an idea. Consequently, they do not invite dialogue. "Reach out and touch someone", if taken literally, might get someone arrested". "You deserve a break today"; but what about tomorrow? "Just Do It" is devoid of context and barren of thought. Does *L'Oreal's* slogan, "because you're worth it" epitomize anything other than narcissism and the illusion that loveliness can be acquired by means of a credit card?

Marshall McLuhan, who spent the better part of his life studying advertising gimmicks, once said that "The business of the advertiser is to see that we go about our business with some magic spell or tune or slogan throbbing quietly in the background of our minds." The slogan can be intoxicating, even if it is not persuasive on a rational level.

Oscar Wilde's *The Picture of Dorian Gray* provided a compelling symbol by which we could understand a larger, cultural problem, namely that people wear masks to conceal their true identities. The advertising executive who speaks only in slogans may very well represent our own cultural tendency to spout things we do not mean to people we do not know for  reasons we do not fully understand. Thus, human relations are supplanted by product purchases. The buyer and the commodity replace the person and his neighbor. The "I-Thou" relationship yields to that of "I-It".

At the polar opposite of the slogan is the prayer. And the whole point of prayer is to establish a dialogue with God. Prayer should never be a monologue. Most assuredly, the purpose of prayer is not to tell God what He must to do for us. According to St. Thomas Aquinas, "It is clear that he does not pray, who, far from uplifting himself to God, requires that God shall lower Himself to him, and who resorts to prayer not to stir the man in us to will what God wills, but only to persuade God to will what the man in us wills."

Let us suppose that one night we are watching television and our program is interrupted by the words, "And now a word from our Creator". What would we do? Would we change the channel? Or simply turn the TV off? Or would we wait in terror? We might turn from the word of God because we fear that it does not coincide with our wants. But God, being God, knows what we *need* better than we do ourselves. And what we need is usually better than what we want. In prayer, then, we must be open to surprises. We speak to God, and He speaks to us. His Will is usually not in our script. But He is Our Father, after all, and wasn't that the way He told people how to pray?

Hans Urs von Balthasar, in his marvelous book that bears the simple title, *Prayer*, reminds us that "The Word of God may well require of me to-day something it had not demanded yesterday; consequently, in order to perceive this demand, I must, in the depth of my being, be open and attentive to the word. No relationship is closer, more rooted in being itself, than that between the man in grace and the Lord who gives grace."

In the dialogue of prayer God invites us to do something that speaks to the core of our being. We should be more trustful to the God who created us than to the advertising agent who deceives us. Prayer, then, is an engagement with the being who created us, but knows and loves us, and urges us to awaken to being the best person it is possible for us to be.

THE IMPORTANCE OF FIDELITY

Pierre Teilhard de Chardin stated** that love is "an affinity of being for being". This apparently simple statement is of fundamental importance for it places love on the plane of reality. It serves as the basis for Martin Buber's notion of the "I-Thou" relationship. For Buber, "I-Thou" is a "primary word". It is the living context in which the "I" becomes more real: "I become through my relation to the Thou; as I become I, I say Thou." In the loving meeting between the "I" and the "Thou," both become more real.

Marriage is a special form of the being-to-being, I-Thou relationship. Sacred Scripture refers to it as a "two-in-one-flesh" intimacy. In marriage, husband and wife give their hearts to each other. This gift is not merely an expression of sentimentality, but one that is essentially real. It is so real, in fact, that the death of a spouse can bring about a profound sense of a loss of being in the surviving partner.

The distinguished psychiatrist, Karl Stern, has observed that the death of a marital partner can often produce a "somatic equivalent" in the mourner. He observed that the illness that claimed one spouse "is not infrequently related to the fatal illness of the deceased. Thus, the widow of a man who died of cancer of the prostate may develop a non-specific cystitis. The widower of a woman who died of cancer of the large bowels will develop some form of enteritis."

The case of Richard and Joan Flutie lends confirmation to Stern's observations as well as to the intense realism of an "I-Thou" love relationship. Dick and Joan met in high school and, according to friends, remained together ever since. In October, 2015, they celebrated their 56th year of marriage. Their union resulted in four children, nine grandchildren, and three great-grandchildren. The following month, on November 18th, Richard Edward Flutie died at age 76 in hospital of a heart attack. Less than an hour later, his wife, Joan Marie (Rhoades) Flutie died of an unexpected heart attack at 73 years of age, while saying her final goodbyes in the hospital. Their funeral took place on November 23 in Melbourne, Florida at Our Lady of Lourdes Catholic Church. "They say you can die of a broken heart," commented their son, Doug, "and I believe it."

The news of the passing of Dick and Joan would not have received the broad publicity it has received had it not been for their illustrious son, Doug, who gained fame as a football player, winning the Heisman Trophy while quarterbacking Boston College and then adding to his stature while playing for a quartet of National Football League teams and three Canadian teams earning the honor of "Best football Player in CFL History". After his retirement from football, Flutie established the "Doug Flutie, Jr. Foundation for Autism" in honor of his son. This non-profit organization has raised many millions of dollars for a better understanding and improved treatment of autism.

Doug's dad, despite his career as an aero-space engineer, took the time to mentor his son's athletic development. "My parents were always there for their children," the football legend told the press, "from the days my dad coached us as kids and my mom would work the concession stands. The most important part of their 56 years of marriage was providing opportunities to their children. They were incredible parents and grandparents and my family and I will miss them both."

The Mayo Clinic affirms that the "broken heart syndrome," more technically known as cardiomyopathy, can be brought about by the death of a loved one. But here, medicine is simply corroborating what we know through experience and our awareness that love involves a being-to-being relationship. "To love at all," writes C. S. Lewis, is to be vulnerable. Love anything, and your heart will certainly be wrung and possibly be broken." This should not discourage people from loving because, for Lewis, the only alternative, the logical consequence of refusing to love, is "damnation".

"The only place outside of Heaven," he writes in *The Four Loves*, "where you can be perfectly safe from all the dangers of perturbations of love is Hell."

"Heart," according to the Bible, refers to the whole person. Pleasure pertains to a part of us, like warming our hands before the fireplace. Love demands the wholeness of our being. Love enlarges us, though it does make us vulnerable. Christ died on the Cross of a broken heart because He loved us. As He said to Peter and the two sons of Zebedee, "My soul is deeply grieved, to the point of death; remain here and keep watch with Me" (Matthew 26: 37-38). According to theologian Nicholas Wolterstorff, Christ died of a broken heart: "Let me suggest that Jesus died from stress-induced cardiomyopathy as a result of the rejection and grief he experienced as he walked the world."

The passing within an hour of Mr. and Mrs. Flutie is both sad, since death always saddens us, and inspirational, for it brings to the mind of the public a testimony that love, especially marital love, can be real, lasting, joyful, and productive. It had special personal significance for my wife and I since, on November 18, 2015, we were celebrating our 48th wedding anniversary and thinking about the fruitfulness of those years in which 5 children and 12 grandchildren have come into being. Marriage and the family will forever remain as the basic unit of society.

THE IMPORTANCE OF GRATITUDE

Wherever there is a movement, there are sure to be extremists. Environmentalism offers us a case in point. Perhaps the most outlandish of the environmentalist extremist groups is the one founded by the pseudonymous Les U. Knight. It is called, the Voluntary Human Extinction Movement (VHEMT). The philosophical principle that undergirds this group is the notion that the earth would be better off without humans. Therefore, humans should stop breeding. Its homepage reads as follows: "Phasing out the human race will allow Earth's biosphere to return to good health." Human beings, consequently, should "unite," not to breed, but to become extinct.

Members of VHEMT prefer to read Genesis backwards, moving from the first human beings back to an unpopulated Eden. Apparently, God did not know when to stop. The "apple of God's eye," as Scripture often refers to him, would no longer be man, the creature made in His own image, put the literal apple. The apple, as well as the Earth, would belong to themselves. Yet, in the absence of consciousness, health would no longer be of any value. Nature itself is serenely indifferent to whether it is healthy. In fact, "health" would cease to have meaning. Are the incandescent stars "healthy"? Are tidal waves a sign of health? Are volcanic eruptions better off when there are no human being around? The plain truth is that intelligence must be present in order to ascribe "health" to anything. Nature is unaware of its health, beauty, violence, or chaos. Without consciousness, the universe remains incomplete.

"Keep me as the apple of your eye," sings David in *Psalm* 17:8. The psalmist is happy to be part of a world that is characterized by relationship, one in which nothing is closed in on itself. God creates man out of his generosity and places him in an environment that sustains his life. The apple symbolizes life, nourishment, beauty, and immortality. Man exists

167

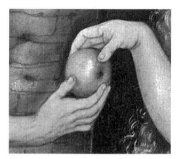 for God and the apple tree for man. The entire universe comes to be and evolves as a result of each ingredient making its contribution to another. The astronomer, Carl Sagan, who authored the popular television series, *Cosmos*, reminds us that the world is a network of innumerable particles all working together through giving and receiving, when he makes the flowing observation" "If you wish to make an apple pie from scratch, you must first invent the universe." The apple, indeed, has a long lineage.

We sit down to enjoy a slice of apple pie and thank God for creating the apple. We may also thank Him for the extraordinary versatility he has given to this special fruit. And consider the glorious array of desserts it has generated, from turnovers to tarts, crumbles to cobblers, strudels to sauces, hot and cold ciders, jellies, butters, pancakes, and apple pan dowdies. Thanksgiving is the grateful remembrance that God created an orchard and was most eager to share it with us. Gratitude is as appropriate to God's creation as applause is to a good performance.

According to legend, the apple caught the arrow of William Tell and the noggin of Sir Isaac Newton. For Milton, it tempted Adam and Eve, for Steve Jobs, it inspired new horizons for the world of computers. It was the dramatic symbol in the tale of Snow White. It is the sobriquet of America's largest city. It was the vocation of Johnny Appleseed. It is Halloween's treasured emblem. It pleases the teacher and keeps the doctor away. And so, Henry David Thoreau could rightly observe "how closely the history of the apple tree is connected with that of man."

If the fig tree remains barren, it should be cut down (*Luke*, 13:6-9). To give or to bear fruit is needed for the universe to unfold as it should. The Ebenezer Scrooges of the world are an anomaly. Christmas is for men of good will. Mother's milk is for the baby. Pregnancy prepares the continued life of the child. Abortion is anti-evolutionary, unnatural, and regressive. In the *Song of Solomon* (8:5), we find an interesting association between the apple and the fruit of a mother's womb: "Under the apple tree I awakened you. There your mother was in labor with you; there she who bore you was in labor." Human birth takes place in the context of fruit-bearing nature. The earth is a home in which we find ourselves mirrored. Returning to the *Song of Solomon* (2:3), we read: "Like an apple tree among the trees of the forest is my beloved among the young men. I delight to sit in his shade, and his fruit is sweet to my taste."

The apple belongs to the tree only while it is being nourished. When it is ripe, it belongs to us. So too, with respect to the relationship between a mother and her child in the womb. Timing and generosity are the hallmarks of creation and life. Nature is a great teacher and is prodigious. We can count the number of seeds in an apple, but only God can count the number of apples that can be generated from a single seed.

The fact that the apple belongs to us, and not to the tree, reassures us of God's generosity and his creative presence, and the essential importance for human beings to order their lives through giving and receiving. Thanksgiving, then, is an opportunity for us to offer thanks to God for making apple trees, and to grandma for making mouth-watering apple pies.

THE IMPORTANCE OF COURAGE

Early in his *Confessions* (Book I, Chapter 6), St. Augustine raises a question that is rich in existential implication and, at the same time, sheds important light on the human condition: "What have I to say to Thee, God, save that I know not where I came from, when I came into this life-in-death—or should I call it death-in-life?" Augustine expresses his amazement, as we all might, over the fact that he exists as a unique human being not knowing how he came to be and what may be asked of him. He speaks for all of us, we individual human beings who stand outside of nothingness and, not through our own designs, nonetheless exist, have consciousness and can question how and why we are here.

In referring to the polarities of "life-in-death" and "death-in life," Augustine is alluding to the unalterable human condition. We would prefer life to be detached from any trace of death and strive mightily to achieve that condition — sex without tears, life without toil, wealth without work, choices without regret. But we are haunted by the death factor and cannot break loose from it. St. Augustine is telling us that human existence is a mosaic of life and death, and, consequently, that our only choice is between "life-in-death" and "death-in life".

The pre-Socratic philosopher, Heraclitus gave a name to this tendency to move between opposites. He called it *enantiodromia* (*enantios*, opposite, and *dromos*, a quick movement). Nothing is fixed. Life is a contest of opposites: birth and death, health and sickness, hope and disillusionment, giving and taking, day and night, summer and winter, love and hate. In fragment 62 he writes: "Immortals, mortals; mortals, immortals; our life is their death and our death is their life." In his dialogue *Gorgias*, Plato repeats the words of Euripides: "Who knows whether living is not dying and whether dying is not living?" "If anything is constant in the history of mankind," states the cultural historian Erich Voegelin, "it is the language of tension between life and death."

The perpetual question for human beings is whether they should find "life-in-death" or, failing that, lapse into "death-in-life". T. S. Eliot struggled with that question and it is the central theme of his poem, *The Waste Land*, considered by many scholars as the most important poem in the English language of the 20th Century. The poem's epigraph foretells the theme that Eliot weaves in a style that is both prolific as well as perplexing. It refers to the prophetess Sybil who had been granted any wish she desired. In her haste, she chose immortality, or life without death, rather than eternal youth. As a result, she continued to shrink as she aged until she was diminutive enough to fit into a small jar. In a voice that was barely audible, she cried out, "I want death".

For Eliot, the Waste Land is inhabited by people who prefer death to life. This is what is implied in the poem's opening line: "April is the cruelest month." April, of course, signals the beginning of Spring, and with it, the regeneration of life. But the people of the Waste Land prefer death and find, in their bleak situation, nothing but death. Water, symbolizing that which gives life, and rock, symbolizing authority, are both lacking. What life can emerge, Eliot writes, "Out of this stony rubbish? And the dead tree gives not shelter, the cricket no relief, And the dry stone no sound of water."

The eminent literary scholars F. R. Levis and F. O. Matthiessen see Eliot's masterpiece as involving a tension between two kinds of people, those of a Christian type who see life-in-death, and a secular type who see death-in-life. For the Christian, Easter follow Good Friday. For the secularist, there is no resurrection, and death, not life, becomes the predominant factor of human existence. The Christian lives by the supernatural virtues of faith, hope, and charity. The secularist falls back on sensuality, stupefaction, and superstition. Novelist John Updike has eloquently captured the futility of Eliot's death-in-life mood when he makes the following insightful remark: We live in "one of those dark ages that visits mankind between millennia, between the death and rebirth of gods, when there is nothing to steer by but sex and stoicism and the stars." Literary critic Cleanth Brooks, Jr., in his analysis of *The Waste Land* makes the comment that "men dislike to be aroused from their death-in-life". Claire Olivia Miller's 1974 study is entitled, *The Waste Land: T. S. Eliot's Search for Life-in-Death.*

Saint John Paul II, in his encyclical, *Evangelium Vitae* (The Gospel of

Life) draws attention several times to the conflict in the contemporary world between a Culture of Death and a Culture of Life. If we look at the encyclical in Augustinian terms, we see that at the root of this clash is the existential choice on the part of individual human beings to prefer a "death-in-life" mode of existence to that of a more Christian "life-in death" approach. While it is palpably true that there is a contemporary clash between the Cultures of Life and the Cultures of Death, we should attach responsibility not so much to the two cultures as cultures but to the collective choices made by individual persons.

The tradition from Augustine to John Paul II is telling us that human existence is an unbreakable dyad of life and death. The purpose of our existence is to find life in death, while resisting the dark temptation of seeing death as its dominant feature. St. Augustine had sampled the bitter taste of death-in-life. His conversion, as it is for all of us, is in finding joy and meaning in the experience of life in death.

174

THE IMPORTANCE OF HOLINESS

W e speak of the church as being a "holy place," the liturgy as Holy Mass, and a saintly person as being "holy". Holiness has a broad application though its many uses derive from a consistent meaning. The notion of holiness may be easier to recognize in a person than it is to define in words. One recalls how the multitudes recognized the holiness of John Paul II and exclaimed in one voice, "*Santo subito*" (sainthood now). Nonetheless, it is possible through the medium of writing, rather than through the medium of a holy person, to shed some light on this most exalted and important quality.

We begin by looking to language. Holiness, as its etymology in almost every European language indicates, is a special form of wholeness. The words "heal," "health," "whole," and "holy" are all etymologically related. A person may be healed and regain his health, which is his physical wholeness. But holiness is a form of wholeness that includes God. As such, it involves man's conformity to the will of God. Holiness, therefore, is a complete form of wholeness.

For St. Thomas Aquinas, holiness signifies two things. First, it denotes "purity," which means being "unsoiled". In this regard, holiness implies a certain intimacy with God, a union without alloy. Aquinas is well aware that the human mind can be "soiled" by its involvement with pleasures and possessions. Secondly, for the Angelic Doctor, holiness denotes "firmness" inasmuch as it demands loyalty to God who is both man's beginning and end. In general, holiness refers to both the person of holiness and God to whom and for whom the person's actions are directed (*Summa Theologica* II-II, 81, 8).

Holiness is original. The holiness of God precedes all other forms of holiness, just as innocence comes before guilt, and as Creation comes before the Fall. In not remaining holy, one is rejecting his original condition. John Henry Cardinal Newman, in one of his sermons, speaks of "the holy and renewed heart which God the Holy Ghost gives us" and "how it may exist in infants, who obey the inward law without knowing it, by a sort of natural service, as plants and trees fulfill the functions of their own nature; a service which is most acceptable to God, as being moral and spiritual, though not intellectual." Newman's remark is consistent with the appropriateness of identifying the male children who were slaughtered by King Herod as the "Holy Innocents."

Another important application of the adjective "holy" is in reference to the "Holy Family". The family had a long history before the advent of Christianity. But, as G. K. Chesterton has astutely observed, Christianity "did not deny the trinity of father, mother, and child. It merely read it backwards, making it run child, mother, father. This it called, not the family, but the Holy Family" (*Heretics*, 1905). Giving the child prominence distinguished the holy family from *pater familias* (Latin for "father of the family" or "owner of the family estate"). By the unselfish pouring of their love into the child, parents imitate the procession of the Holy Trinity that gives prominence to the Christ-child and special honor to the Nativity. Abortion, therefore, is a clear and emphatic refutation of a family's claim to holiness.

Because holiness is original, it is not ambitious. A person of holiness is not interested in performing heroic acts but in doing everything with a purity of heart. Purity, then, is maintaining one's original condition. St. Peter affirms the qualities of purity and firmness in his own way in *I Peter* 1:13-16 where he states the following: "Therefore, prepare your minds for action, keep sober in spirit, fix your hope completely on the grace to be brought to you at the revelation of Jesus Christ. As obedient children, do not be conformed to the former lusts which were yours in your ignorance, but like the Holy One who called you, be holy yourselves also in all your behavior; because it is written, 'You shall be holy, for I am holy'" (see also *Leviticus*, 11:44 and 19:2).

Holiness is recognizable because it imparts a splendor of its own, naturally, and without fanfare. A lighthouse does not ring bells, send up flares, or shoot off cannons in order to communicate its presence. It simply shines. Holiness is profoundly and effectively communicative on its own terms. This is what Blaise Pascal had this in mind when he stated that "The serene silent beauty of a holy life is the most powerful influence in the world, next to the might of the Spirit of God."

One of the most unfortunate features of the modern world is the dethronement of God and the enthronement of man in his place. By virtue of this usurpation, man takes on the task of defining and generating his own holiness, a feat that is not possible since holiness is not the mark of one who is alone and alienated from God. Thus, the atheist philosopher, Friedrich Nietzsche could advise, "Love yourself through grace, then you are no longer in need of your God, and you can act the whole drama of Fall and Redemption to its end in yourself."

With the concomitant eclipse of God and decline of religion, it is no longer commonly believed that God is an eternal and inextinguishable source of wisdom and goodness, that God alone is the measure and the means of all holiness. Instead, man himself, not God, becomes the measure of all things. But it is God that remains the measure of His creation and not his creatures.

Holiness belongs primarily to God. Whatever degree of holiness an individual possesses does not originate within himself but through his intimacy with the Divine. Holiness is not an illusion; it is an objective reality apparent in the life of one who radiates the love of God.

CHAPTER NINE
LIVING A LIFE OF FREEDOM

FREEDOM AND FULFILLMENT

I n his 1971 opus, *Freedom in the Modern World,* Jacques Maritain states that "a prime error which seems to be at the root of many of our contemporaries" is to make freedom of choice "the highest form of freedom". The distinguished French philosopher was not thinking specifically about America at the time he penned his discourse on freedom, but the attention he drew to this error is directly relatable to the problem that has had a most deleterious effect on American society for several decades.

In responding to a question regarding how he would preserve "reproductive rights" in a speech he gave to the Planned Parenthood Action Fund on July 17, 2006, Barack Obama declared, "The first thing I'd do, as president, is sign the Freedom of Choice Act. That's the first thing I'd do". The Freedom of Choice Act grants a woman the "right" to abort at any time prior to the viability of the fetus and any time after that if continued pregnancy is necessary to protect her life or her health. It also authorizes an individual who is aggrieved by a violation of this act to obtain appropriate relief in a civil action.

Although, the Freedom of Choice Act has not been passed, a woman's freedom of choice to abort remains virtually sacrosanct. Maritain is at pains to point out that freedom of choice, which is most certainly a good and worthy power, is not man's highest freedom and should be subordinated to a freedom of fulfillment that gives value and meaning to freedom of choice. In other words, freedom of choice, is not man's highest freedom nor is it an end in itself. It exists for something greater than itself, namely a freedom of fulfillment by which a person becomes more complete as a person.

Freedom of choice is our birthright. The charge that pro-life people are "anti-choice" is both erroneous as well as slanderous. No one is truly anti-choice in this sense. No one is lobbying that human beings should be turned into zombies who are bereft of the freedom to make choices. Our capacity to choose freely is natural, like having arms and legs. But the critical point, overlooked by "pro-choice" advocates, has to do with how we use the various powers that nature has bequeathed to us.

An analogy between baseball and life may serve to clarify the point. A runner is on first base with no outs. The batter has a certain freedom of choice. He may try to bunt the runner to second base, attempt to hit behind the runner, or swing away. But his freedom of choice is understood entirely with respect to how his choices help to win the game. He is not free to make any choice that comes into his head. He is not free to strike out deliberately, since this use of freedom does not advance the cause of the greater freedom of winning the game. Each choice a player makes through the contest is predicated on how it stands to help bring about victory. It is victory that is architectonic. No one is urging that every action in the game should be self-justifying. What justifies the action is how it relates to winning. Therefore, freedom of fulfillment is not only higher than freedom of choice, but determines the very meaning of each individual act of choice.

The important question is not whether we are "pro-choice" or "anti-choice" but how can we use our naturally given freedom of choice to help bring about our freedom of fulfillment? What methods of practicing does a violinist use in order to become a virtuoso? How do we choose so that our choices add up to meaning? The answer involves the use of reason that enlightens us about where our choices are likely to lead us. It is something like using a map to get us to our destination. The map illuminates the various choices we must make in order to reach our destination. If we reject the map and make choices willy-nilly, we find that we are lost. In such an event, our freedom of choice has not served us. Devoid of an end and a basis in reason, freedom of choice, as Maritain points out, "tends merely to dissipate in indefiniteness and indecision".

If there were but one point of enlightenment I would want to share with my ethics students it is that the essence or the formal element of freedom of choice is not freedom itself, but reason. We have freedom of choice to begin with. We get the best from that power by making a reasonable use of it. The so called "anti-choice" people are really not "anti-choice" but "pro-reason". We may behave reasonably or unreasonably. The problems we create for ourselves are largely the result of a misuse of reason. It is "consonance with reason," as St. Thomas writes, which is the formal constituent of moral action. Making freedom of choice self-justifying obliterates all distinction between good and evil, right and wrong. If freedom of choice reigns supreme, then the most egregious acts against human dignity and justice become acceptable.

Pro-choice enthusiasts, including President Obama, disvalue the very power they eulogize. By making choice an end in itself, they fail to see how regulated acts of free choice can bring about a better person and a better world. They lack vision, have not sense of the possibility of gradual improvement. They have no life strategy and burn themselves out by making heedless choices that have resulted, for many women who chose abortion, in deep regret. Pro-life enthusiasts, on the other hand, love freedom of choice because they understand how many such choices, arranged in an evolving manner, can lead to a fulfillment that mere freedom of choice is unable to provide.

FREEDOM AND CULTURE

The late Ronald Dworkin (1931-2013) was a prominent and influential scholar of United States constitutional law and jurisprudence. In his book, *Life's Dominion: An Argument About Abortion, Euthanasia, and Individual Freedom* (1993) he states that "Abortion, which means killing a human embryo, and euthanasia, which means killing a person out of kindness, are both choices for death." We may set aside his inaccurate description of all those who are aborted as "embryos," and his assumption that people are euthanized out of "kindness," and give him credit for providing a direct object for a person's "choice". Those who call themselves "pro-choice" are usually squeamish about identifying exactly what their choices bring about. Dworkin is bold enough to say that abortion and euthanasia choices result in death. In this single sentence, he succinctly and accurately encapsulates our present moral climate as a Republic of Choice within a Culture of Death.

In this same work, his enthusiasm for the freedom that choice represents, allows him to state that "Abortion chooses death before life *in earnest* has begun; euthanasia chooses death after it has ended." It would seem that Dworkin's enthusiasm for freedom has given him license to invent a new characteristic of a developmental stage of the unborn, while denying the all too obvious fact that only those whose lives have *not* ended are eligible for euthanasia. There is no biological basis for asserting that at one stage, the fetus is not developing "in earnest," and at another stage it is. As a matter of fact, the cellular development of the unborn is more prolific than it is at any other stage of life. After age forty, the human organism plateaus, so to speak, or, in Professor Dworkin's terminology, no longer continues "in earnest". Moreover, euthanasia ends a life; it does not bring death to a subject that is already dead.

Unbridled freedom (or unrestricted choice) has a peculiar consequence. It generates its opposite. Too much air causes the balloon to burst, thus, causing it to lose all its air. When stretched too far, the rubber band snaps, thereby becoming tensionless. Before we sit down to feast on our new found freedom, however, we should examine the collateral effects that that unbounded freedom produces. Dostoevsky warned many years ago that "Boundless liberty leads me on to boundless tyranny." His is a warning that should not go unheeded. A single, isolated value—freedom—cannot produce a balanced society.

The word "enantiodromia" (*enantios*, meaning "opposite" + *dromia*, meaning "running" is a term that was originally used by ancient Greek philosophers. It refers to the phenomenon of something turning into its opposite. It found an important place in the psychology of Karl Jung. The motion picture *The Lives of Others* (2006) offers an example of enantiodromia to illustrate how a person devoted to a communist regime can break out of that mould to become a humanist of an altogether different stripe.

An ongoing development in Canada exemplifies how too much choice can lead directly to denying choice to others. The majority report of the Special Joint Committee on Physician-Assisted suicide reflects an acute sensitivity to the plight of those who are suffering. What its members seem less sensitive to is the importance of safeguards that would prevent euthanasia from becoming what some have called "a new medical growth industry". The report is a recommendation that Canada's Criminal Code be amended to allow physicians, nurses, nurse practitioners, and pharmacists to put people to death. The suffering could be either physical or mental, terminal or non-terminal. Moreover, the Report states, in three years euthanasia could be extended to "competent mature minors" of any age. Therefore, euthanasia could be extended to a wide range of subjects as well as to a wide range of "assistants". This range, according to the Report, could also include those suffering from poverty or social isolation. Even those who are not suffering in any way, could make themselves eligible for euthanasia through advance application for their deaths. All publicly funded hospitals would be required to offer these services.

If Parliament accepts the recommendations of the Joint Committee, Canada would take its place on the forefront of euthanasia along with the Netherlands and Belgium. Among a number of critical questions that can be raised involves the freedom of choice of those who work within the medical profession and do not want to assist in the death of another person. This question also applies to institutions, especially Catholic hospitals, whose mandate is directly opposed to killing people.

If euthanasia in Canada does become something like a growth industry, this would mean that fewer members of the medical profession who oppose assisted killing would be allowed to act in accordance with their conscience. One person's choice could violate another person's conscience. Such a situation would logically discourage conscientious people from entering the world of medicine in the first place. Secular society becomes more efficient when there is uniformity of opinion, where everyone agrees on the reigning ideology of the day. However, this Orwellian nightmare, that is intolerant of reasonable dissent, is a way of mechanizing health care and losing sight of the dignity of both the patient and the health care worker. In such an environment, Ronald Dworkin's assertion that euthanasia is an act of kindness seems stretched to the breaking point. A Culture of Death has little patience with the afflicted. It is not a kindly act to kill someone, nor is euthanasia a branch of health care.

FREEDOM AND NATURE

Certain thinkers of the past, whose minds were more in love with theory than with practice, believed that birds could fly faster in a resistance-less medium, that is, in a vacuum. Without the air to push their wings against, as we now know, birds would not be able to fly at all. They would also need oxygen to take in so that they could remain alive. The point here is that, although the temptation exists to increase freedom beyond its natural boundaries, freedom is conditioned. In a nutshell, there is no liberty without truth, just as there is no justice without truth.

And so, too, marriage is conditioned. People do have a right to marry, but it is not absolute. The right to marry is conditioned by several factors including: a) obtaining the consent of the other, b) that both parties are unmarried, c) that the other is not a blood relative, and d) that the other is a member of the opposite sex. Would marriage "fly" better if any or all of these conditions could be removed? Or can we say that these conditions do not restrict marriage, but define it, give it its nature, and distinguish it from other types of relationships?

Justice Anthony Kennedy, is supporting same-sex marriage in the *Obergefell v. Hodges* ruling, argued that "the right to marry is a fundamental right inherent in the liberty of the person . . . couples of the same-sex may not be deprived of that right and that liberty." Here, Justice Kennedy is treating marriage as if it were an unconditional right, which it is clearly is not. This is the same Justice who stated in the 1993 *Planned Parenthood v. Casey* decision that "At the heart of liberty is the right to define one's own concept of existence, of meaning, of the universe, and of the mystery of human life." The fact that no American government has ever opposed a person's "right" to have his own concept of the "mystery of human life," raises the question of the judicial significance of Kennedy's words. In his book, *Slouching Towards Gomorrrah*, Robert H. Bork contends that Kennedy's words "were intended, through grandiose prose, to appeal to a free-floating spirit of radical autonomy."

Kennedy, along with four other judges believed that the Constitution allowed them to excise the male/female condition from marriage and thereby give it greater life. But if the Majority could do this, could it not also strip marriage of its incest and pedophilia taboos, and of it opposition to bigamy and polygamy, and even of its freedom of consent requirement? It is not possible, as the four dissenting justices agreed, to find in the Constitution a proviso that allows the pruning of marriage. Chief Justice Roberts stated that the Majority simply acquiesced to a preference: "The truth is that today's decision rests on nothing more than the majority's own conviction that same-sex couples should be allowed to marry because they want to, and that 'it would disparage their choice and diminish their personhood to deny them this right.'"

Lino Graglia, a professor of law at the University of Texas, puts America's attitude concerning the Constitution over the past forty years or so into perspective when he states the following: "[T]he thing to know to fully understand contemporary constitutional law is that, almost without exception, the effect of rulings of unconstitutionality over the past four decades has been to enact the policy preferences of the cultural elite on the far left of the American political spectrum."

The migration from a judicial role to a political one has made it evident that judges in general, and several members of the Supreme Court in particular, do not operate out of a realistic grasp of the nature of things. Liberty (or freedom) for we human beings is always conditioned. We are not free-floating, autonomous creatures. Nor is marriage an institution with no definable boundaries. In his 1993 encyclical *Veritatis Splendor*, Saint John Paul II explained in great detail how liberty cannot be dissociated from law. It was a caveat, to no one's surprise, that was unheeded by the Majority. The Pontiff Emeritus noted that "some present-day cultural tendencies have given rise to several currents of thought in ethics which center upon *an alleged conflict between freedom and law*. These doctrines would grant to individuals or social groups the right *to determine what is good or evil*. Human freedom would thus be able to 'create values' and would enjoy a primacy over truth, to the point that truth itself would be considered a creation of freedom."

The Court set aside the reality of marriage, its nature and truth, and in a mood of freedom, conferred upon it new meaning. The Court, therefore, claimed to achieve a metaphysical impossibility — using judicial fiat to transform an objective reality. But marriage cannot fly when its wings are clipped. That is to say, marriage ceases to be marriage when part of its essence is removed. Neither individual persons nor the United States Supreme Court have the power to create new verities to replace old ones.

Justice Clarence Thomas, in dissent, is right when he points out that "liberty," in the American tradition, "has long been understood as individual freedom *from* governmental action, not as a right to a particular governmental entitlement." We are less free when the government imposes its will on us. It is worth noting that the 1973 *Roe v. Wade* decision denied the unborn their natural right to life and made their continued existence conditional on the mother's choice, whereas they denied the conditional right to marry and treated as if it were a natural right. We have good evidence to believe the words of Robert Bork when he advises us that "There is no particular reason to think that people with Ph.D.s are more well-intentioned than people who dropped out of high school."

FREEDOM AND LIFE

On April 14, 2016, Canada's Liberal government introduced Bill C-14 legalizing euthanasia and assisted suicide. The long-awaited draft is intended to amend two Criminal Code sections that formerly prohibited euthanasia and assisted suicide. The Supreme Court of Canada, in a 9-0 decision on February of 2015, declared these sections to be unconstitutional.

While there will be further discussion before the draft proposal becomes law, the Catholic Bishops of Canada have strongly denounced it, stating that "no matter how it will be amended" it remains a "danger to all vulnerable persons — particularly the aged, disabled, infirm and sick who so often find themselves isolated and marginalized."

Of special concern to the bishops is that the proposed federal bill contains no explicit protection of conscience rights. As the bill presently stands, the Liberal government will leave it up to provincial and territorial governments to decide whether or not publicly funded health centers will be compelled to provide euthanasia and assisted suicide. Toronto's Cardinal Thomas Collins has implored the government not to "force or compel in any way either an individual or an institution to facilitate their wish against the conscience of the person or the institution". He stressed the critical importance of making palliative care available for all. "At a time when our priority should be fostering a culture of love, and enhancing resources for those who are suffering," he stated, "assisted suicide leads us down a dark path".

The title of this brief essay, "Liberty without Freedom," is not meant to be a contradiction in terms, although these two nouns are often used interchangeably. When we take a careful look are "liberty" and "freedom" we find a very important difference between them. "Freedom" is meant to complement "liberty". But it is possible for an excess of liberty to become freedom's enemy.

Liberals love liberty far more than they love freedom. In fact, it may be said, observing what has transpired in Canada and the United States over the past few decades, that liberals hate freedom and are happy to crush it wherever possible. This point may make more sense once we analyze the difference between liberty and freedom.

The word "liberty" is derived from the Latin *libertas*, which means "unrestricted, unbounded, or released from constraint". It is consistent with the notion of being separate and independent. On the other hand, the word "freedom" can be traced to the Germanic or Norse word *Frei*, describing someone who belongs to a tribe and has rights that go with such belonging. Therefore, it contains a communal implication that *libertas* does not have. Moreover, *frei* is the root word for "friend".

When viewed in this light, it becomes clear that liberty and freedom should be complementary and not antagonistic to each other, just as the individual person should fit smoothly into society.

Alexis de Tocqueville, in his most perceptive work, *Democracy in America*, warned about an excessive preoccupation with liberty. "I think that liberty," he wrote, is endangered when this power is checked by no obstacles which may retard its course". His understanding that too much liberty can crush freedom is made more evident when he stated that "I hold it to be an impious and an execrable [extremely bad] maxim that, politically speaking, a people has a right to do whatsoever it pleases." As Dostoevsky once remarked, "Unbounded liberty leads to tyranny."

De Tocqueville was cautioning young America that removing one restriction after another so that individuals can do what they please, undermines their freedom to do what is right for their nation. Some restrictions, codified in law, serve as protections. Restrictions on speeding protect motorists and pedestrians. Restrictions on shoplifting protects business. By removing restrictions that really protect the common good constitutes a threat to society. We need liberty ("freedom *from*," to use Erich Fromm's terminology), so that we can enjoy "freedom *for*".

By removing the restriction on abortion, a woman has the liberty to abort. But her liberty comes at the price of destroying the freedom of her unborn child as well as the freedom of the father to protect his unborn child against premature death. As a result of removing the restriction that marriage is a union between a man and a woman, the freedom not to officiate at same-sex marriages has been denied to certain magistrates.

And now, removing restrictions against euthanasia and assisted suicide may very well violate the consciences of medical professionals as well as patients who do not want to die. Instances of forced euthanasia are well documented in the Netherlands and Belgium.

Liberty, of course, has a positive function. The restrictions that enslave a person must be removed so that he can take his rightful place in society. Here, liberty exists *for* freedom. But the restrictions that require him to refrain from criminal activity must be upheld, and also for the good of society. When too many restrictions are withdrawn, society descends into chaos, what Thomas Hobbes referred to as "a war between all against all". Legitimate restrictions are needed so that law can function. When restrictions that serve to protect are removed, law no longer exists to protect people against themselves.

Archbishop Richard Smith of Edmonton is acutely aware of how too much liberty, that is, the removal of too many restrictions, is tantamount to an assault on the freedom of citizens and sets them up as victims of discrimination. "What is already clear," he states, "is that this legislative step [in Canada] introduces into law the chilling message that some lives are less worth living that others."

Liberty should not crush freedom; nor should it discriminate against people. Rather, it should prepare the way and provide the opportunity for freedom. "With liberty and justice for all," means that the limits of liberty are set by the demands of freedom.

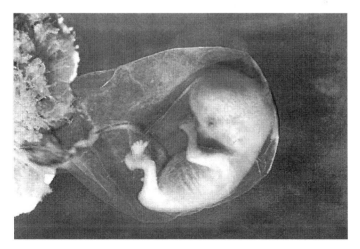

FREEDOM AND LIBERTY

These proud words of Samuel Francis Smith changed the opening stanza of "God Save the Queen" to that of "My Country 'Tis of Thee," though the music of these two songs remained identical. The latter became America's de facto national anthem until it was replaced by "The Star Spangled Banner," which was recognized for official use by the United States Navy in 1889.

Apart from their patriotic glow, these words raise some interesting philosophical questions: 1) Do "liberty" and "freedom" have the same meaning? 2) Are "liberty" and "freedom" ends in themselves? 3) Is there a proper ordering between "liberty" and "freedom"?

In June of 1888, Pope Leo XIII produced his encyclical "On the Nature of Human Liberty". It was a carefully reasoned argument against that form of "liberalism" in which the individual human being claims that he has the right to decide for himself the norms by which he should regulate his life. "The true liberty of human society," the Holy Father wrote, "does not consist in everyman doing what he pleases, for this would simply end in turmoil and confusion." He argued that liberty should never be severed from reason for "on the use that is made of liberty the highest good and the greatest evil alike depend." United with reason, liberty it can open the way to truth; separated from reason, it can open the way to error. "It is contrary to reason," Leo XIII concluded, "that error and truth should have equal rights".

Liberty, then, is not an end in itself. It emancipates a person from restrictions that would otherwise hinder him from pursuing his rightful end. Herein is it value. But, despite his liberty, a person remains free to pursue ends that are contrary to his rightful end. He may sing of liberty, but mourn in infamy.

The Revolution of 1776 liberated America from England. Under President Lincoln, the "Emancipation Proclamation" liberated blacks from slavery. The "Woman's Liberation" movement removed certain obstacles, cultural and economic, that held women back. Liberation, understood as the removal or restrictions, has played a prominent role in American history.

The notion of responsibility, however, has not earned as enthusiastic a reception in the story of America. Citizens of the United States do not sing of their "Sweet Land of Responsibility". When the distinguished psychiatrist Viktor Frankl visited the United States, he advised that the Statue of Liberty on the east coast should be counterbalanced by a Statue of Responsibility on the west coast.

The word "liberty" teems with optimism and often carries the Pelagian implication that people will always use it well. We celebrate liberty long before we know how we will use it. Yet, as history shows only too plainly, the misuse of liberty has often led to tyranny. Marx, Hitler, Lenin, Stalin, Mao Tse-Tung promised liberation but delivered tyranny. The word "liberty" is charged with promise, though its bright hopes are not always realized. Liberty is light; responsibility is demanding.

Karol Wojtyla (later saint John Paul II) published his book *Love and Responsibility* in 1960, the inaugural year of the turbulent sixties when America's youth was playing out love and irresponsibility. It is responsibility that prevents liberty from advancing to license, and its resulting in chaos and confusion. Yet responsibility does not seem to be glamorous, theatrical, or particularly patriotic. The fact that many women used their newly found liberation to embrace contraception, abortion, sexual promiscuity, and easy divorce offered proof that liberty is not an end in itself and needs reason, guidance, and a sense of personal responsibility in order for it to remain faithful to what is good. We need more than liberty to become whole persons.

"Liberty" is not the same as "freedom" even though these words are often used interchangeably. Liberty, as we have seen, carries the implication of removing restrictions. Freedom, on the other hand, has two fundamentally different meaning. It can mean "freedom of choice" or it can mean "freedom of fulfillment".

Freedom of choice, from a moral point of view, is highly ambiguous. One may choose good or evil. If a person is liberated from undue restrictions, he is free to choose. But if he is to choose what is good, his choice must be guided by reason. Freedom of choice is not an end in itself. But it is a pre-condition or a prelude to choosing what is good. In choosing what is good, a person enjoys what we may call a "freedom of fulfillment". This personal fulfillment is an end in itself for it represents the end or even the perfection of the person. Freedom of choice exists for freedom of fulfillment. Jacques Maritain states the matter as follows in *Freedom and the Modern World*: "It is our duty by our own effort to make ourselves persons having dominion over our own acts and being to ourselves a rounded and whole existence. There we have another kind of Freedom, a freedom to gain which we must pay a great price: Freedom in fulfilment."

We need to be liberated from hindering restrictions. Therefore, though only up to a point, liberty is good. We need freedom of choice to choose what is good. But choice is subservient to what is good. Therefore, we need freedom of fulfillment to crown the distinctive uses of liberty and freedom of choice.

When we peel an orange, we "liberate" the pulp from the skin. In order to be nourished by the orange we must not throw it away, though we are free to do that, but consume it. In this homey example, we follow the sequence of liberation, freedom of choice, and freedom of fulfillment.

CHAPTER TEN
LIVING LIFE ON THE HORIZON

DESTINY

"**V**erizon," the name of the electronic communications giant, is what is called, in sophisticated circles, a "portmanteau" word. It is a hybrid of two words fused together like "Internet" which is the blending of "International" and "Network". "Motel" (motor + hotel), "televangelist" (television + evangelist), and "brunch" (breakfast + lunch) are popular examples of portmanteau words. The two words that make up "Verizon" are "*verus*" and "horizon". "Verizon" is a bold hybrid that suggests that there is a bright future on the horizon and that it belongs to the world of electronic communications.

But if "Verizon," though extremely well-marketed, is not our true horizon in any moral sense, we are left to ponder what our true horizon might be. The distinguished theologian Hans Urs von Balthasar once remarked that every family should have a "hearth" and a "horizon". Traditionally, the mother had the role of the former, the father, the role of the latter. Today, however, uncompromising egalitarianism is loath to attach specific roles to men or to women. We have lost sight of our horizon and seek meaning in the "Now". As a result, we have lost a way of connecting the present with the future. Our moral compass does not seem to be pointing in any particular direction.

Christianity brought into the world what now seems to be a lost horizon. We have become immersed in the immanent. We have lost our way and no longer know what road to take. As Dag Hammarskjold has written, "Never look down to test the ground before taking your next step; only he who keeps his eye fixed on the far horizon will find the right road." This loss of a larger vision seems to be evident in the current attitude toward marriage and divorce.

Christ made it clear enough when speaking to the Pharisees that marriage is indissoluble: "Have you not read that he who made them from the beginning made them male and female, and said, 'For this reason a man shall leave his father and mother and be joined to his wife, and the two shall become one flesh'? So they are no longer two but one flesh. What therefore God has joined together, let no man put asunder" (Mt. 19:3ff; Mk. 10:2ff.). The Pharisees, as do many Catholics today, found this to be a hard saying. But Christ repeated that "from the beginning it [divorce] was not so" (Gen. 1:27). The Pharisees were well aware that Moses allowed divorce, but Christ told them that it was because of "the hardness of heart" that Moses allowed divorce. Christ was not downgrading the importance of the moment. He wanted to set it in the context of a larger perspective so that it would not obscure the distant horizon. It was the *true* horizon that Christ had in mind.

The Pharisees believed in the here and now, in comfort and convenience. Christ was insisting that their vision was insufficiently narrow to see the horizon toward which He wanted them to direct their lives. Contraception was accepted in the modern world because it promised a more comfortable life and greater convenience for the moment. But it opened the door to abortion, same-sex marriage, and various forms of euthanasia. It had a devastating effect on both the integrity and the very meaning of marriage and the family.

The English essayist Clive Bell examined sundry civilizations from ancient Greece to Enlightenment France and concluded that no great civilization ever placed comfort ahead of more important values. The commitment to comfort is not an effective strategy for the long road. We have sentimentalized marriage and feel sorry for divorced Catholics who want to remarry. But Christ is not being legalistic or insensitive when He teaches that marriage is indissoluble. He knows that the loving bond of matrimony is of critical importance for the good of the spouses, for the proper care of children and for the benefit of society. As the family loses is integrity, the government becomes, more and more, the formative principle of society. Sentimentality leads to easy divorce, adultery, instability, neglect of children, and political oppression. Because sentimentality lacks a horizon, it fails to see things in their larger implications.

Sentimentality, succumbing to emotions rather than employing reason, is both myopic and inconsistent. The sentimentalist is in love with "compassion," but he has wounded that word by cutting it off from any horizon that would give it its true significance. The late essayist Joseph Sobran was right on the mark when he made the following statement: "What is strange—at least at first sight—is that this callousness about the unborn child should occur in a society where we are forever hectored to show 'compassion' for others. Even as enlightened voices urge us to take responsibility for unseen strangers, they soothingly release us from responsibility to our own children." For Malcom Muggeridge, compassion is "a beautiful word now so abased as to be unuseable."

In *Ephesians* 4:13, St. Paul advises us to be "tender-hearted". This is a most interesting word. It contrasts with the hard-hearted people of Moses' time, and yet St. Paul does not use it to advocate sentimentality. In *Corinthians* I: 15, St. Paul urges us "to be watchful and stand firm in the faith, be manful and stout-hearted." Our hearts should be tender enough to accept God's Word and to forgive others. At the same time, they should be stout-hearted enough to carry on God's Word and not collapse under social pressure.

We should not lose sight of our true horizon or submit to secular or technological horizons that are mere fabrications. Hearth and horizon connect the present with the future, the immanent with the transcendent, and the temporal with the eternal. Life is always larger than what it seems to be in the moment. Christ wants us to live on that larger and more rewarding plane.

DIVINITY

An aphorism is a brief statement, usually containing a piece of practical wisdom. It is not as witty as an epigram, as noble as a proverb, or as overused as an adage. It is closer to the maxim, which, according to Mark Twain, "consists of a minimum of sound and a maximum of sense." A maxim, however, differs from an aphorism in that it is always a short rule for moral conduct, such as "look before you leap". Ralph Waldo Emerson, that quintessential American whom Oliver Wendell Holmes believed to have personified "America's Declaration of Independence," was most adept at writing aphorisms. One of my favorites that flowed from the pen of this ordained Unitarian minister is the following: "All that I have seen teaches me to trust the Creator for all that I have not seen. "This statement is sufficiently rich in philosophical and theological implication that it warrants analysis. It bears more wisdom than the eye might see at first glance.

Suffering and death were close companions of Emerson. Three of his siblings died in childhood. His father passed away two weeks before the young Emerson's eighth birthday. Two of his bright and promising younger brothers died early in life of tuberculosis. His wife, Ellen Louise Tucker, also succumbed to the same disease, at age twenty, just two years into their marriage. His aforementioned aphorism, therefore, is not something he wrote off the top of his head. Indeed, it came from a heart that understood well how people who have suffered deeply could question God's love.

Emerson speaks to all of us. We all see things that give us a sense of God's presence. At the same time, we see things that cause us to question why He allows so much suffering in the world. But Emerson does not merely "see," in the conventional sense of the term, he sees *through* things to another world. In his first published essay, "Nature," he makes the following statement: "Nature is a language and every new fact one learns is a new world; but it is not a language taken to pieces and dead in the dictionary, but the language put together into a most significant and universal sense. I wish to learn this language, not that I may know a new grammar, but that I may read the great book written in that tongue."

Emerson saw the book of nature as authored by the Creator. St. Thomas Aquinas saw nature as a reflection of the Eternal Law, a notion not very much different than Emerson's view. Nature is diaphanous, something through which we can see something else. The eighteenth century poet William Blake made reference to this when he drew a distinction between seeing *with* the eye and seeing *through* the eye:

> This life's dim Windows of the Soul
> Distorts the Heaven's from Pole to Pole
> And lead you to believe a Lie
> When you see with, not thro', the Eye.

Seeing only *with* the eye is to see nothing more than matter. It is simply a glance. But to see *through* the eye is to see what exists beyond the realm of mere nature. Malcolm Muggeridge compared his conversion into the Catholic Church with the blind man whose sight Jesus restored: "Whereas I was blind, now I see" (*John* 9:25). "How [could I] have not understood," he writes in his book that bears the simple title, *Jesus*, "that the grey-silver light across the water, the cry of the sea-gulls and the sweep of their wings, everything on which my eyes rest and my ears hear, is telling me about God." For Muggeridge, his new vision allowed him to pass from what he referred to as a "kingdom of fantasy to the kingdom of reality."

The book of nature is, as Emerson tells us, something that "teaches" far more than biology can. It teaches us that there is a trustworthy God who operates through nature. We need that special vision of seeing *through* the eye to sense His existence. But God's being, seen through all the wonders of his creation, is seen as a God whom we can trust. The God of beauty must be a God of trustworthiness. Another poet, William Wordsworth, spoke of nature being "apparelled in celestial light." That "light" originates from a Being that transcends nature, but makes His presence known through nature.

Finally, the Rev. Emerson, recognizes that he is unable to judge the Creator he has never met. This is what gives added depth to his aphorism. Though we may be hurt, crushed, devastated by the loss of loved ones, we are in no position to judge the God we cannot see. There is nothing in nature that implies the existence of an untrustworthy God. We can rejoice when we sense God's presence, and humbly bow our heads when we do not understand. Gerard Manley Hopkins struggled to comprehend why God would allow five Franciscan nuns to perish aboard the *Deutschland*. "For I greet him the days I meet him, and bless when I understand," he wrote in his most dramatic poem, "The Wreck of the Deutschland". When we do not sense God's presence, we do not understand, and must withhold judgment. God knows what we cannot know. "Thou art lightning and love," Hopkins remarked. We rejoice in the love, and should remain silent about the lightning.

OPPORTUNITY

One of the most improbable ways of getting a fire started is by using ice. That's right, using *ice*. No survivor's manual would be complete without describing how this can be accomplished. First, one finds some clear ice and then shapes it into a disk that can be used as a lens. The lens serves as a magnifying glass that captures rays of sunlight which can be directed to dry leaves, kindling wood or some other kind of tinder, and presto . . . a fire is started. This method serves as an example of how resourcefulness can overcome a situation that seems utterly hopeless.

Inconvenience can be irritating. But inconvenience comes in degrees. On Saturday, January 23, 2016, dozens of buses were stranded on the Pennsylvania Turnpike. The massive amount of snow that had fallen made it impossible for them to move. Here is inconvenience multiplied exponentially.

But it did not cause pro-lifers, who were trying to return home after they had participated in the annual March for Life, to despair. A group of Catholic students from Omaha and Minneapolis-St. Paul suggested that all the stranded pilgrims celebrate Mass. Even without a survivor's manual, some of the pilgrims took things into their own hands and made a serviceable altar out of ice and snow. Word spread throughout the stranded buses. One priest had 300 or so hosts. Six priests gathered themselves and con-celebrated Mass for, in round numbers, 500 people.

Resourcefulness means knowing what to do when there seems to be nothing that one can do. The fire of the Holy Spirit no doubt emerged from the icy altar, illustrating once again, that hope can arrive when everything appears to be hopeless and that one can produce fire from ice, even theologically. Mary magnified the Lord, a more glorious magnification than the shaped ice that magnified the rays of the sun.

Resourcefulness is the virtue of the poor. Betty Smith, in her celebrated novel, *A Tree Grows in Brooklyn*, describes the resourcefulness of the Nolan family that had to use considerable ingenuity just to scrape by. It was amazing what the mother could do with stale bread! She would pour boiling water over a loaf, work it up into a paste, flavor it with salt pepper, thyme, minced onion and an egg (if eggs were cheap), and bake it in the oven. When the concoction was good and brown, she would thicken it with flour and add two cups of boiling water, seasoning, and a dash of strong coffee. What was left over was sliced thin the next day and fried in hot bacon fat. It was not a meal fit for a king, but it did provide taste and nourishment.

Just because a door is closed does not mean that it is locked. As someone once said, "It is better to try and fail than to fail to try." We can look to the humble bumble bee as an image of resourcefulness. Scientists have concluded that this wonder of God's creation, from the standpoint of aerodynamics, cannot fly. Yet, in tune with its own inner resourcefulness and despite its ignorance of science, it flies nonetheless. God has supplied each one of His creatures with an inner capacity for resourcefulness that enables them to function and to flourish.

In the motion picture, *Cast Away*, Chuck Noland (played by Tom Hanks) is plunged into the Pacific Ocean when his plane goes down as a result of a violent storm. He manages to escape the plane and is saved by an inflatable life raft. Thanks to his resourcefulness he is able to survive on an uninhabited island. After a great deal of struggle and pain, he sets himself adrift on a raft of his own making and is finally picked up by a cargo ship. His ordeal and return to civilization parallels our own struggles and our hope to return to God's Kingdom. Chuck Noland is Everyman.

The character of *Cast Away* emerges from his proving ground a better man. Prior to his plane flight he was married to his schedule. He breaks off Christmas with his beloved so that he can catch a plane. In checking his watch, he decides he has enough time—five minutes—to open his gifts in the car on his way to the airport.

We are all castaways, cast away from our finally destiny in this world of inconvenience and trouble. The stranded pro-lifers, though momentarily cast away from their homes, did not lose joy or hope. The Holy Family was cast away from the inn and Christ had to be brought into the world amidst cattle and straw. Our affluent society offers us a convenient answer to every inconvenience we might experience. We have instant coffee, fast food restaurants, automatic money machines, high speed Internet, and an assortment of time-saving devices. Commercial advertising is constantly offering us new products that promise to make our lives easier. Yet we must question whether these products stifle our resourcefulness, that inner compass that directs us to overcome inconveniences with ingenuity. We may also question whether a world of artificial inconvenience is robbing us of our patience and causing us to sleepwalk through life.

Hats off to the stranded pro-lifers whose resourcefulness has reminded us of our exiled condition and our need to be resourceful as well as hopeful and joyful. Their victory over ice and snow brings warmth to our hearts. We speak of natural resources. But the most natural, as well as the important of all resources is the indefatigable human spirit.

IDENTITY

Before *Roe v. Wade*, but when the abortion issue was being hotly contested, certain pro-life leaders in Canada, as well as in the United States, told me that once people realized what abortion entails the controversy would be settled solidly in favor of life. The plausible assumption in the minds of these leaders was that people based their moral decisions purely on the basis of information. Abortion, however, involving, as it does, life, parenthood, responsibility, and personal liberty, is far too profound an issue to be settled on the basis of information alone. And although all the information pertinent to abortion is on the side of life, the will can be a formidable opponent when it comes to changing people's minds. Abortion is not simply an intellectual issue it involves the will, a human faculty that can be intensely recalcitrant.

C. S. Lewis makes it clear to his readers that his conversion was anything but a simple matter. In *Surprised by Joy* (Chapter 14), he offers the following vivid personal account. "You must picture me alone in that room at Magdalen, night after night, feeling whenever my mind lifted even for a second from my work, the steady, unrelenting approach of Him whom I so earnestly desired not to meet. That which I greatly feared had at last come upon me. In the Trinity Term of 1929 I gave in, and admitted that God was God, and knelt and prayed: perhaps, that night, the most dejected and reluctant convert in all England."

Conversion to God parallels converting to life since God is pre-eminently Life. The will can be more stubborn than a mule. Nonetheless, the will always retains its natural inclination toward the good. Where there is will there is hope. In his exceptionally insightful treatise, *The Conversion of Augustine*, Romano Guardini makes the comment that "conversion can only be something that seizes a man with a life-or-death grip."

We are all victims, to varying extents, of sleepwalking through life. We need something extraordinary to jar us out of our slumber. Those who remain unconverted are headed for a terrible fate, as Shakespeare warns in Macbeth: "To-morrow and to-morrow and to-morrow creeps in this petty pace from day to day to the last syllable of recorded time and all our yesterday's have lighted fools the way to dusty death."

The realism of Guardini's remark came home to me with great force one night after I had given a pro-life presentation. As I walked to my car, I heard a voice calling out to me. The rapid pace of the caller's footsteps communicated to me a sense of urgency. I stopped and greeted a rather serious looking young man who was most eager to tell me something. He introduced himself quickly and gracelessly. It was his story he wanted to impress upon me. And so, we stood in the parking lot under a slight drizzle of rain while he unravelled his extraordinary tale. It was to be a far more important revelation than the meager message I had delivered minutes earlier.

My friend had been in Uganda for several years doing peace work as an emissary of the Canadian government. Because of political unrest in Uganda, the Canadian government advised him to leave that country as soon as possible. His life was at stake. He boarded a train that would transport him out of a country where foreigners were suddenly in imminent danger. Little did he realize that his train-ride would be fraught with a different and more terrifying kind of danger. A soldier approached  him, pointed his machine gun at him, and told him that he could blow him away and no one on the train would care. He could then toss his dead body out the widow and into the jungle where no one would ever find him. My friend was in the grip of terror, accompanied by an experience of complete isolation and alienation. He was utterly alone and completely at the mercy of another person's arbitrary will. Whether his life continued or ended had nothing to do with human rights but teetered on the whim of a total stranger. He was guilty of nothing other than the fact that he existed. Yet this seemed to be a crime large enough to sentence him to his premature demise. There was nothing he could do to lobby for his life. It was power versus helplessness. The cat and mouse game went on for approximately a half-hour. As time went on, as my friend explained to me, he felt more and more confident that he would not be shot.

After what must have been the longest thirty minutes of his life, the soldier moved away. My friend would continue to live. He had been re-born. But he had also been transformed. During the ordeal in which he was helpless, unable to plead his case, and completely at the mercy of another, he identified with the unborn. He had survived his living nightmare in the damp, womb-like environment of a moving train. He underwent a conversion and was re-born pro-life. He emerged from his "life-or-death grip" with an enlightened appreciation for life. His conversion occurred at a moment when life was not safely separated from death but was brought into close proximity with it. It was in this tangle of life and death that he knew, with uncommon clarity, how much life is preferable to death.

For Christians, the Cross unites life with death and conveys the timeless message that life is not to be taken for granted but to be lived with gratitude, gladness, and generosity.

LEGACY

The name Clare Boothe Luce is one that should not remain absent from the minds of contemporary Catholics. She may not have been a saint, but was vitally concerned about how much a saint can do to restore a backward culture. She understood only too well that in times of crisis we need saints. In 1952 she edited a classic entitled, *Saints for Now*. It was a compilation of twenty essays written by twenty distinguished authors (mostly Catholic) about their favorite saints and how much these servants of God meant to the times in which they lived. In her Introduction, Mrs. Luce made the following comment: "We live in an intellectual climate of ambiguity, of multiple and conflicting 'truths,' of exclusive and warring 'freedoms.' In a world where truth is relative, where one man's 'truth' is another man's 'lie,' and his definition of 'freedom' is his neighbor's definition of 'slavery,' plainly the burden of carrying the argument . . . must fall on an appeal not to the mind, but to the emotions. Advertising, propaganda—the sophisticated tools of irrationalism—supersede fact, persuasion and logic, the tools of reason." Pulitzer Prize winner, Phyllis McGinley reiterated the point in *Saint-Watching* when she stated that "Ours is an age of violence and disbelief. But in spite of that, or because of it, the earth's interest in virtuous accomplishment is stronger now than it has been at any time since the Age of Reason began ousting religion from its seat of authority."

The "now" that Luce described better than six decades ago and McGinley lamented seventeen years later seems an apt description of the "now" of 2015. *Plus ça change, plus c'est la même chose* (The more things change, the more they stay the same). Three questions leap to mind: Are cultures always confused and divided? Is it futile to insist on reason and logic? Who are the saints of today that will rescue culture from ruin? McGinley believes "They may well be rising among us now, preparing to lead us out of the onrushing night which so threateningly descends." The "now" should not be dissolved by the following moment in time, but should be prevented from passing into oblivion by connecting it with what is timeless. This is the office of the saint.

Clare Luce was led into the Church by Fulton Sheen and was often referred to as America's most famous Catholic convert. Her talents were various and prodigious. She was a novelist, a playwright, editor, essayist, philanthropist, member of Congress, diplomat, and Ambassador to both Italy and Brazil. The opening night of her play, *Margin for Error*, which is an all-out attack on the Nazi's racist philosophy, was attended by Albert Einstein and Thomas Mann. Several of her plays were adapted to the screen. In 1983 President Reagan awarded her the Presidential Medal of Freedom. She was the first member of Congress to receive this award.

She was a critic of her times (and, prophetically, of the current times as well). Yet, she understood how difficult it may be to shed one's prejudices and think objectively and rationally. On one occasion, she confronted her house guest, the renowned philosopher, Mortimer Adler, who, staring blankly at his feet, seemed bored. When she asked him if there was something he would like to do, noting her puzzlement, he explained: "I'm thinking. And that's the hardest thing in the world, because, you see, when you really want to think a question through, you've got to begin by laying all your prejudices on the table. And that's the toughest thing for anyone to do, even for a philosopher." In 1980, Dr. Adler wrote, *How to Think About God: A Guide for the Twentieth Century Pagan*. His lifelong preoccupation with thinking was not unfruitful. At the age of 97, two years before his death, he entered the Catholic Church. "Finally," wrote his friend, Ralph McInerny, "he became the Roman Catholic he had been training to be all his life."

In a 1977 issue of *The Human Life Review*, Clare Boothe Luce reminded the world that "no Supreme Court ruling is considered infallible". It was an important message she left to posterity. As she went on to explain, "historically the Court has been prone to reflect the political mood (and emotional prejudices) of the public, and as the mood changed or new facts emerged, the Court has often reversed itself . . . as in the case of the *Dred Scott* decision, the Court's decision has been reversed by amendment to the Constitution when it ceased to reflect a public consensus."

It is hard to set aside one's prejudices, even for members of the Supreme Court, and to think objectively, fairly, and without prejudice. Mrs. Luce would not be astonished, if she were alive today, at the recent *Obergefell* decision. It is a continuation of mankind's penchant for allowing emotions, the temper of the times, fashions and trends, to interfere with judicious thinking. We need hard thinkers like Sheen, McGinley, Adler, McInerny, and the redoubtable Clare Luce Boothe. But even more, we need saints.

The distinguished playwright one remarked that "Courage is the ladder on which all the other virtues mount." There can be no sanctity without courage, the courage to stand against contemporary prejudices and hold firm to what is true. Moreover, there can be no virtue without courage, and a culture without virtue is indeed destitute. And what is sanctity? It is, as Phyllis McGinley avers, and Mrs. Luce would most certainly endorse, "the world's strangest and highest form of genius." Culture should welcome such geniuses as the music world embraces Bach, Beethoven, and Brahms. But first, culture must lay aside its own prejudices and open itself to truths that transcend time.

Clare Boothe Luce passed away on October 9th, 1987 at the age of 84. She is buried at Mepkin Abbey, South Carolina, a plantation that she and her husband, Henry Luce, had given to a community of Trappist monks. May her legacy and their prayers be a source of healing for our battered times.

Other Titles by Dr. DeMarco

- *Abortion in Perspectiv*
- *Sex and the Illusion of Freedom*
- *Today's Family in Crisis*
- *The Anesthetic Society*
- *The Shape of Love*
- *The Incarnation in a Divided World*
- *In My Mother's Womb*
- *Hope for a World without Hope*
- *Chambers of the Heart*
- *How to Survive as a Catholic in a Parochial World*
- *Character in a Time of Crisis*
- *The Many Faces of Virtue*
- *Timely Thoughts for Timeless Catholics*
- *New Perspectives in Contraception*
- *The Integral Person in a Fractured World*
- *Patches of God-Light*
- *The Heart of Virtue*
- *Virtue's Alphabet from Amiability to Zeal*
- *Biotechnology and the Assault on Parenthood*
- *Architects of the Culture of Death*
- *Being Virtuous in a non-Virtuous World*
- *The Value of Life in a Culture of Death*
- *A Family Portfolio in Poetry and Prose*
- *How to Flourish in a Fallen World*
- *In Praise of Life*
- *How to Remain Sane in a World That Is Going Mad*
- *Ten Major Moral Mistakes and How They Are Destroying Society*
- *Poetry That Enters the Mind and Warms the Heart*

HOW TO REMAIN SANE
IN A WORLD THAT IS GOING MAD

Donald DeMarco

TEN MAJOR
MORAL MISTAKES
And How They Are
Destroying Society

Donald DeMarco

Poetry That Enters
the Mind and
Warms the Heart

A Collection of Poems
by
Donald DeMarco

Each accompanied by the author's commentary

Made in the USA
Columbia, SC
22 March 2023

14143399R00124